HISTORY AND HISTORIANS

Seventh Edition

HISTORY AND HISTORIANS

A Historiographical Introduction

Mark T. Gilderhus

Texas Christian University

Prentice Hall
Upper Saddle River, New Jersey 07458

Library of Congress Cataloging-in-Publication Data

Gilderhus, Mark T.
 History and historians : a historiographical introduction / Mark T. Gilderhus. — 7th ed.
 p. cm.
 Includes bibliographical references and index.
 ISBN-13: 978-0-205-68753-4 (alk. paper)
 ISBN-10: 0-205-68753-9 (alk. paper)
 1. History—Philosophy.   2. Historiography.   3. History—Methodology.   I. Title.
D16.8.G533 2009
907.2—dc22

2008051988

VP, Publisher: Priscilla McGeehon
Executive Editor: Charles Cavaliere
Project Manager (Editorial): Rob
 DeGeorge
Editorial Assistant: Lauren Aylward
Executive Marketing Manager: Susan
 Westmoreland
Marketing Assistant: Ashley Fallon
Production Manager: Kathy Sleys

**Composition/Full-Service Project
 Management:** Shiji Sashi/Integra
 Software Services
Printer/Binder: Bind-Rite,
 Robbinsville/Command Web
Cover Design: Bruce Kenselaar
Cover Illustration/Photo: Library
 of Congress

Pearson Education Ltd., London
Pearson Education Singapore, Pte. Ltd
Pearson Education, Canada, Inc.
Pearson Education–Japan
Pearson Education Australia PTY,
 Limited

Pearson Education North Asia, Ltd.,
 Hong Kong
Pearson Educación de Mexico, S.A. de C.V.
Pearson Education Malaysia, Pte. Ltd.
Pearson Education, Upper Saddle River,
 New Jersey

Prentice Hall
is an imprint of

10 9 8 7 6 5
ISBN 13: 978-0-205-68753-4
www.pearsonhighered.com   ISBN 10: 0-205-68753-9

*To my daughters Kirsten and Lesley,
my granddaughters Della and Morgan,
and my grandson Jake*

PREFACE

This brief book presents a survey of Western historiography from ancient times to the present. It also shows how historians have grappled with the past in a search for meaning and how history as a body of knowledge has served different goals and purposes among different people in different places and times. Practical considerations require the emphasis on the written narratives of Western civilization. For one reason, preliterate people all over the world have affirmed and maintained their sense of history with unwritten, oral accounts carried on from one generation to the next. These traditions constitute the domain of anthropologists and for the most part reside outside the bounds of this book. In addition, the other two great written historiographies, the Chinese and the Muslim, date respectively from around the time of Confucius in the sixth century BCE and from the death of the Prophet Muhammad in the seventh century CE. These voluminous accounts record the Chinese quest for order and hierarchy in conformance with Confucius's teaching and also follow the expansion of the Muslim faith and the ensuing struggles and conflicts both within and without their world. Obviously, an attempt to reflect upon these histories would introduce a host of cultural and language difficulties. Such an endeavor also would make this short book longer and costlier and would exceed by unimaginable margins the author's knowledge, understanding, and capabilities. Readers with an interest in such things can begin with an essay by David Morgan, "The Evolution of Two Asian Historiographical Traditions," Chapter 1, in *Companion to Historiography*, edited by Michael Bentley (New York: Routledge, 1997), and see the accompanying bibliography.

This seventh edition does incorporate various changes. The material on "Reading, Writing, and Research" no longer takes up space in the book itself but it is available to instructors in PDF format for class use. It can be downloaded from Pearson's online catalogue at www.pearsonhighered.com. Select "Educators" from the menu options and follow the instructions labeled "Download Instructor Resources." Also, the editing process has streamlined the text by removing some examples and illustrations while adding others when appropriate. The results should sharpen the thematic focus and enhance accessibility. The new edition also introduces additional commentary on recent historiographical tendencies and trends, especially in areas concerned with "the cultural turn," "world history," "subaltern studies," "postcolonialism," "the weapons of the weak," and the "agency" of persons previously regarded as powerless and oppressed. Following the lead of French theorist Michel Foucault, such approaches pay special heed to the negotiation and distribution of power in human transactions over the whole spectrum of class, gender, and race. In addition, some new books appear in the bibliographies at the end of each chapter.

Finally, after forty years in the classroom, I want to express my thanks to my students over the decades whose curiosity, energy, wit, insight, and humor have kept me on the alert and also to my colleagues at Texas Christian University who make our history department a challenging and sometimes very entertaining place. Ken Stevens, my department chair, provided support and encouragement. A special friend, Emeritus Professor of History Paul F. Boller, regularly makes my day with conversations about books, history, politics, movies, and W.C. Fields. He brings new dimensions of meaning to the terms "gentleman" and "scholar." My wife Nancy, as always, urged me "to get the damn thing done." I also appreciate the contributions of the following reviewers, whose comments made the book a better one: William Caraher, University of North Dakota; Sarah A. Curtis, San Francisco State University; Sharon Hepburn, Radford University; and Maxine N. Lurie, Seton Hall University.

1

AIMS AND PURPOSES

Why bother with the study of history? What possible connections might link an increasingly remote past with our own predicaments in the present? Can stories about other people in other places and other times have meaning in an age of vaulting technology and traumatizing change? Should we as reasonable people who live in perilous times believe that the experiences of others who came before can benefit us? These questions hold more than rhetorical importance. Students of history need to know what they will learn and the effect on their capacity to think and act creatively in the future.

Skeptics have argued that historical knowledge will not provide much help. American industrialist Henry Ford characterized history as "bunk." Although his observation probably says more about Ford's limitations than about history, other luminaries have expressed similar reservations. In the seventeenth century, French scientist and mathematician René Descartes worried that curiosity about the past would result in ignorance of the present. Another Frenchman, François Marie Arouet de Voltaire, a philosopher and historian, described history as "a pack of tricks we play on the dead." He meant the gibe as an appeal for more accuracy in written history. Nonetheless, skeptics might misread it as support for a classic put-down. Historians, critics say, fall into three camps: those who tell lies, those who are wrong, and those who do not know. Even so powerful a thinker as Georg Wilhelm Friedrich Hegel, a nineteenth-century German, complained that the only thing we learn from history is that no one learns very much from history.

Others display greater optimism. In 1989, Francis Fukuyama, a State Department planner and a Harvard-trained expert on the Soviet Union, created a stir by arguing that the termination of the Cold War really marked "the end of history." Drawing upon "philosophy of history" as a means of comprehending the significance of contemporary events, Fukuyama reasoned, "There is some larger process at work . . . that gives coherence and order to the daily headlines." He characterized it in the twentieth century as "a paroxysm of ideological violence," pitting the values of Western liberalism first against "the remnants of absolutism, then bolshevism and fascism, and finally an updated Marxism that threatened to lead to the ultimate apocalypse of nuclear war." The culmination produced "the triumph of the West, of the Western *idea*." As he explained, "What we may be witnessing is not just the end of the Cold War, or the passing of a particular period of postwar history, but the end point of mankind's ideological evolution and the universalization of Western liberal democracy as the final form of human government." The grandiose affirmation provoked responses from both enthusiasts and critics, and the latter gained the upper hand during the following years when the magnitude of racial, ethnic, nationalistic, and religious conflicts, often violent, sometimes genocidal, raised serious doubts. More on the mark, Fukuyama also suggests that observers of and participants in the events of the present day will have trouble understanding much about their world unless they have an understanding of history.[1]

Albert Shanker, the president of the American Federation of Teachers, made a similar point in 1991 while discussing "The Uses of History." During the debate in the U.S. Congress about whether to wage war against Iraq after the invasion of Kuwait in the Persian Gulf, Shanker noted that speakers filled their arguments with references to history:

> Members talked about Socrates and Abraham Lincoln; the Mexican–American War and the Peloponnesian war. . . .They cited St. Augustine and St. Thomas Aquinas, James Madison and Winston Churchill. Some talked about the appeasement of Hitler at Munich and Mussolini in Ethiopia; others about the Tonkin Gulf resolution that led to our deep entanglement in the Vietnam War.

According to Shanker, this ritual functioned not simply as "a way of fancying up their speeches . . . in a Congressional version of Trivial Pursuit" but "to help them think about and explain the decision they were making—to each other and to the American people." Different delegates drew different conclusions but often used history as "a tool . . . to reason and think about the crisis . . . to frame the debate . . . to make clear exactly where they stood." As he observed, "No one could have followed the debates or had an intelligent opinion about the wisest course of action . . . without at least a basic knowledge of history."[2] As the Roman statesman and orator Marcus Tullius Cicero warned centuries ago, "To be ignorant of what occurred before you were born is to remain always child."[3]

The study of history entails baffling epistemological questions. On what grounds can historians demonstrate that they know what they claim? Will reason, logic, and evidence suffice? If not, what else fulfills the requirement? While charged with the task of recording, explaining, and interpreting the human past in truthful ways, historians must also confront their intellectual limitations while interpreting the past. Those surviving artifacts on which historians base their judgments, typically incomplete, messy, contradictory, and susceptible to different forms of understanding, seldom allow for certainty. As humble practitioners with constricted capabilities, historians have to look upon their findings as partial, tentative, and subject to revision or rejection in the future.

They should, nevertheless, take joy in the quest, confident that on occasion they carry out useful and important functions. Historians operating within the cultural traditions of Western civilization often regard the study of history as a way for human beings to acquire self-knowledge. In the eighteenth century, Edward Gibbon, the great English historian of the Roman Empire, sadly described his subject as consisting of "the crimes, follies, and misfortunes of mankind." Though certainly indicative of a doleful state of affairs, his remarks also held forth the possibility of escaping from such conditions through rational inquiry. Transcendence over the past could come about through knowledge. Studying history could make traditional constraints less binding.

Some historians have invoked their discipline as an ethical sanction. Lord Acton, a Victorian Englishman and a devout Roman Catholic, insisted on maintaining "morality as the sole impartial criterion of men and things." He called upon historians to act as arbiters, defending the proper and correct standards with an expectation that the threat of disapproval in the future might discourage bad behavior in the present. Historians should hold malefactors accountable for their misdeeds. Tacitus, a historian of the Roman Empire, took such an approach with the emperors Tiberius and Nero, and others will do the same with Richard M. Nixon, Bill Clinton, and George W. Bush.

Other historians have presumed similarities between the past and the future, suggesting that knowledge of what has taken place will provide preparation for what will come. How to get ready for the unknown has always posed a problem. George Santayana, a Harvard philosopher, asserted early in the twentieth century that people who forget about the past are condemned to repeat it. This utilitarian conception of history saw in it a way of developing strategies for survival. History comprised the recollections of all people. Santayana's belief affirmed that lessons learned from experience could aid in the avoidance of mistakes, pitfalls, and catastrophes in the future.

As a body of knowledge, history has a long and honorable tradition in Western civilization. Although definitions and points of emphasis have changed over time, written narratives have always centered on human affairs and purportedly set forth truths. The claim to truth means merely that historians have some good reason in the form of evidence for believing in the validity of their accounts. Historian Paul Conkin has devised a succinct description: a history is "a true story about the human past."[4] The adjectives "true" and "human" have significance. The quality of "truth" distinguishes history from legend, fable, and myth. Admittedly, the latter might set forth "truths" of a sort but usually not literally. The concern for the human past allows historians to downplay events in nature except when they affect the activities of people. Volcanic eruptions hold an interest mainly when they bury cities such as Pompeii and snowstorms when they impede invasions of Russia.

From ancient times until the present, the inhabitants of Earth have told stories about themselves, their ancestors, and their origins. The Assyrians carved into stone monuments the names and deeds of their kings for everyone to see. The inscriptions also placed curses on transgressors who might deface the artifacts and violate their integrity. The earliest tales dwelt upon extraordinary occurrences characterized as unusual, wonderful, fabulous, frightful, terrifying, or miraculous. They told of spectacular events, often featuring displays of supernatural power in which the gods and the goddesses participated in human affairs and sometimes determined the outcomes. In the present day, such renditions confuse us because, by our standards, they mingle the true with the untrue and the believable with the unbelievable. Nevertheless, they are not necessarily evidence of overwrought imagination or low intelligence in ancient times. Rather, they bear out the historians' truism that different people in different times and places literally see and experience the world differently. They also suggest that divergent conceptions of truth and believability have separated the present from the past.

A view of history more consistent with our own developed in the ancient world when iconoclasts announced their disbelief in traditional oral accounts and insisted on setting the record straight. In Greece, early in the fifth century BCE, Herodotus of Halicarnassus composed the first "critical history" in the Western tradition by writing the "truth" about the Greek wars against the Persians. While writing *The Histories,* Herodotus employed verifiable information, using eyewitness accounts, official records of state, and his own observations. To admirers, he became "the father of history." Ever since, historians have tried to tell true stories about the human past.

For two and one-half millennia, the study of history has satisfied many aims and purposes. Many students of the subject probably acquired an interest out of simple fascination. As curious and inquisitive beings, they enjoyed the sheer fun of vicarious experience while asking, "What was it like?" Through imagination, they could enter into the past and take part in the Punic Wars or the Renaissance. Some reveled in knowing esoteric pieces of information, possibly the kind of armaments used in battle during the Hundred Years' War or the lineage of Swedish kings, while others found in history a source of instruction, that is, a way of making the course of human affairs understandable, or at least some portions of it. As noted by a European folk saying, people are not lost until they do not know where they have been. Historians seek to keep us from getting lost by locating us in time and figuring out where we have been.

Although simple curiosity offers a sound reason for embarking upon historical studies, a strong sense of psychological necessity often provides additional incentive. Teachers and researchers in most fields want to make phenomena intelligible. They need to bring some measure of order and predictability to the world. They dislike disorder and unpredictability because random and haphazard events defy comprehension and may signal danger.

Such vulnerability implies futility and the possibility of extinction. Scholars want to know what likely will happen under various circumstances. Most academic disciplines strive to make accurate predictions about probable outcomes. Such is the case in physics, chemistry, sociology, and political science. It is also true in history, except that there the process takes place backward in time instead of forward. On the basis of fragmentary, imperfect evidence, historians make retroactive predictions, or "retrodictions," about what probably happened in the past and then set forth cause-and-effect relationships that make the flow of events explicable. Whenever historians make cause-and-effect statements—"Americans moved west because of the Panic of 1837"—they affirm their belief in the intelligibility of events in the human world. Things happen for reasons, and inquiring minds can grasp them.

Such assumptions are engrained in the traditions of Western civilization. Whether they are actually true is perhaps less important than the historians' tendency to act on the conviction that they are. For historians traditionally, the identification of cause-and-effect relationships establishes meaning and comprehensibility even though such claims can seldom be proven as literally true. As logical constructs, they have to be taken on a large measure of faith. As an example of an alternate view, Kurt Vonnegut's novel *Slaughterhouse Five* contains an intriguing vignette. The central character, the remarkable Billy Pilgrim, has the capacity to move around in time and space. He can travel into the past, into the future, and also beyond the confines of Earth. In one episode, he is kidnapped by extraterrestrial beings from the planet Tralfamador. They put Billy Pilgrim on public display, locked up in a transparent dome with another captive, Montana Wildhack, a voluptuous movie starlet. The Tralfamadorans enjoy watching the two cavort about and also engage them in philosophical discussions. Billy Pilgrim amuses and awes his captors by affirming his belief that cause-and-effect relationships govern the course of events. Things happen because other things make them happen. The Tralfamadorans have a different notion. For them, things happen merely because they happen—randomly, haphazardly, inexplicably, chaotically. The adoption of any such worldview would make the work of historians almost impossible.

History also provides a way to study human identity among individual persons and groups. In some ways, this function parallels psychiatry and psychoanalysis. Experts in these fields also endeavor to clarify human behavior in the present by making knowledge of the past consciously explicit. Just as psychiatrists and psychoanalysts seek to treat aberrant or disturbed conduct by scrutinizing repressed or unconscious memories, so historians try to obtain a fuller grasp of the actions of people by examining their history. Robin G. Collingwood, a British philosopher and historian, liked to suggest that human beings possess no nature; they have merely history. As malleable creatures, they become whatever their experiences make of them.

Even allowing for exaggeration, Collingwood has a compelling point. Historical experience shapes and molds the identity of people in important ways. Most of us recognize this claim as a fact in our rituals. For centuries, Jewish people in their Passover feasts have told the story of ancient Israel and the special covenant with Yahweh, their God, and have managed, in spite of isolation and dispersion, to maintain a collective sense of group identity. In the United States, Fourth of July ceremonies advance a similar purpose. By invoking patriotic lore about the American Revolution, the celebrants establish a sense of solidarity by commemorating the origins of their nation. Just as a single person might explore the question "Who am I?" by thinking through life experiences, historians tell the life stories of people. When we ask, "Who are the Arabs, or the Germans, or the Sioux?" or "Who are we?" the narratives of history provide one place to begin.

Another reason for studying history is utilitarian and practical. According to this rationale, history has a useful application because it helps us better to calculate the anticipated consequences of our own acts. George Santayana probably had this idea in mind when he said that people will repeat the past if they forget it. His words should not be taken too literally. The Second World War will not happen again, even if we neglect to learn about it. Santayana meant something deeper. He knew that history forms the collective memory of humankind and that the onset of a mass amnesia would have bad effects. For one thing, it would prevent the young from learning from the old. Each generation would have to find fire and invent the wheel once more. Without memory, we would have trouble functioning and making do in the world. What each generation transmits to the next can be understood in some measure as lessons in the art of survival.

Philosopher Karl R. Popper pointed out another facet of the problem. He believed that social scientists and historians should contemplate the unintended consequences of deliberate human acts. Sometimes things go wrong. Historical actors set out to accomplish a set of goals and actually bring about unanticipated or contrary results. Popper wanted students of human affairs to investigate the linkages between intentions and outcomes. Napoleon's attempt to dominate Europe destroyed feudal structures and cleared the way for modernization. The United States employed military force in South Vietnam in defense of self-determination and facilitated the obliteration of a small country. Such ironies, sometimes comic, sometimes tragic, abound in human experience. Theologian, philosopher, and historian Reinhold Niebuhr pondered this maddening issue in his book *The Irony of American History* and warned that the actual consequences of our acts sometimes subvert our commitment to ideals. We need to be careful in pursuing grandiose purposes because so often they go awry. If we could better reckon the relationship between aims and outcomes, we would vastly improve our chances of behaving more constructively in the world.

Historians traditionally have composed their narratives by affirming the existence of cause-and-effect relationships and appraising the connections among the actions of historical figures, their presumed motives, and the actual consequences. The following three-stage model of historical inquiry has descriptive, not prescriptive, importance. It shows how some historians carry out their work but sets forth no requirement that they must proceed this way.

During the first step, historians begin their inquiry by asking, "What happened? How did the historical actors behave? What did they do?" This part is the easiest. As long as some kinds of artifacts exist, such as oral traditions, stone tablets, manuscripts, diaries, newspapers, or official records of state, historians can arrive at some determinations. If no remnants of the past exist at all, then no written history is possible.

During the second step, historians must account for the actors' behavior by asking the question "Why?" The answer usually calls for an explanation or interpretation and has tricky implications because it entails an assortment of methodological and theoretical dangers. Historians traditionally have employed a "rational human" model of behavior in framing their responses. They have assumed that most people set rational goals for themselves and then seek to achieve them through the exercise of reason and logic. In more recent times, dissenters have criticized this approach as hopelessly antiquated. Marxist scholars have argued that economic and class relationships usually determine behavior, no matter what the pretext, and that ostensibly principled and righteous actions often emanate from hidden purposes aimed at self-aggrandizement. Similarly, the advocates of psychohistory have rejected the "rational human" model. In their efforts to apply psychoanalytical theories to history, they find the wellspring of human behavior not in reason and logic but in repressed impulses tucked away deep within the recesses of the psyche. In recent times, no matter what the ideological trappings, advocates of postmodernism understand human activity primarily as a quest for power over others. Such disparities mean that discussions of motive are always tentative and uncertain.

In the final step, historians try to evaluate the consequences of events. They ask, "How did things turn out, for good or for ill? Who benefited and who suffered? Did the outcome make the effort worthwhile?" On such big and significant questions, historians seldom agree. The reason is obvious. Any attempt to address them will draw upon different and rival value systems, that is, divergent standards of judgment for which no means of reconciliation exist. How can historians accurately measure the costs and gains of the Mexican Revolution after 1910? About one million people died out of a population of twelve million. If these events had never occurred, would "progress" by peaceful means have made Mexico a better place at less expense? Similar questions arise in discussions of all forms of revolutionary activity. Indeed, they form one of the constants in the historiography of the French Revolution. Honest scholars have to admit that they have no good way of knowing for sure. Was the Second World War really "the good war"? Was the use of two atomic bombs truly necessary? Among other things, history involves its practitioners in an ongoing and sometimes irresolvable debate over the meaning of human experience.

Historians practice their craft in a kind of intellectual minefield in which all sorts of unknown and unanticipated dangers pose threats, and the best of projects can blow up before them. The evidence often is too sparse to tell the whole story. Even when it exists in abundance, the difficulties of explanation, interpretation, and evaluation are immense. Yet historians persist in their toil, seeking to render some small portions of human experience intelligible. This book is a short introduction to the practices and patterns of historical thinking within the context of Western civilization.

RECOMMENDED READINGS

Engaging observations and pungent definitions of the nature of history appear in Ferenc M. Szasz, "The Many Meanings of History," *History Teacher,* 7 (Aug. 1974), 552–63; 7 (Nov. 1974), 54–63; 8 (Feb. 1975), 208–16; and another piece provided by subscribers, 9 (Feb. 1976), 217–27. Introductory works considering aims and purposes include Fritz Stern, ed., *The Varieties of History: From Voltaire to the Present* (New York: William Collins Publishers, 1956); Allan J. Lichtman and Valerie French, *Historians and the Living Past: The Theory and Practice of Historical Study* (Arlington Heights, IL: AHM Publishing, 1978); Carl G. Gustavson, *The Mansion of History* (New York: McGraw-Hill, 1976); and Arthur Marwick, *The Nature of History* (New York: Dell Publishing, 1970). R. G. Collingwood, *The Idea of History* (New York: Oxford University Press, 1956), although difficult for beginners, is indispensable. Karl R. Popper's essay "Prediction and Prophecy in the Social Sciences," appears in the collection edited by Patrick Gardiner, *Theories of History* (New York: Free Press, 1959), 276–85. Useful reference works with names, terms, definitions, and bibliographies include *The Routledge Companion to Historical Studies* (New York: Routledge, 2000) by Alun Munslow and *Fifty Key Thinkers on History* (New York: Routledge, 2000) by Marnie Hughes Warrington. Other extended commentaries on the nature of history include David Lowenthal, *The Past is a Foreign Country* (New York: Cambridge University Press, 1985) and Joseph Mali, *Mythistory: The Making of Modern Historiography* (Chicago: University of Chicago Press, 2003). Various essays in *The French Revolution: Recent Debates and New Controversies* (New York: Routledge, 1998), edited by Gary Kates, considers the discussion over the costs and gains. Finally, the *Companion to Historiography* (New York: Routledge, 1997), edited by Michael Bentley, a 997-page compendium, provides a comprehensive survey of historical thinking from ancient times until the present. For a historiographer, it is indispensable. Two books by Beverley Southgate, *Why Bother with History?* (New York: Longman, 2000); and *What Is History For?* (New York: Routledge, 2005) contain cogent comments on topics suggested by the titles.

ENDNOTES

1. Francis Fukuyama, "The End of History," *National Interest* (Summer 1989), 2–18; idem *The End of History and the Last Man* (New York: Free Press, 1992). Criticism of Fukuyama's views appears in Keith Windschuttle, *The Killing of History: How a*

Discipline Is Being Murdered by Literary Critics and Social Theorists (Paddington, Australia: Macleay Press, 1996), 159–73.

2. Albert Shanker, "Where We Stand: Debating War in the Persian Gulf and the Uses of History," *New Republic* (Feb. 1991), 7.

3. Quoted in "Senator Robert Byrd Speaks Out on the Teaching of American History," *OAH Newsletter*, 29 (May 2001), 3.

4. Paul K. Conkin and Roland N. Stromberg, *The Heritage and Challenge of History* (New York: Dodd, Mead and Co., 1971), 131.

2

THE BEGINNINGS OF HISTORICAL CONSCIOUSNESS

The traditions of Western civilization incorporate distinctive forms of historical consciousness and understanding. These developed from the legacies of the Jews, Greeks, and early Christians. A full account appears in John Burrow's witty, insightful, and quite wonderful book, *A History of Histories: Epics, Chronicles, Romances and Inquiries from Herodotus and Thucydides to the Twentieth Century* (2008), especially Chapter 11, "General Characteristics of Ancient Historiography." The Jews and Christians derived from past events a sense of meaning, structure, and process. For them, history merged with the present and the future and moved inexorably toward a set of knowable goals. The Greeks, meanwhile, insisted upon studying history critically and scientifically in efforts to determine the truth. For them, the distinction between history and mythology became fundamental.

In contrast, the earliest human beings probably had scant historical consciousness. They lived in an expansive present in which the urgencies of mere survival pressed incessantly upon them. Indeed, the terrors of the past—the recollection of impermanence, hunger, death, catastrophe, and destruction—may have created psychological barriers against the act of remembering. The trauma of mere existence drained meaning from past events, except perhaps the negative connotations. To whatever extent the earliest people conceived of a time dimension, their impressions probably took on a cyclical form, that is, a conception of events moving more or less pointlessly in a circle. Things occurred, went away, and then recurred, following the pattern of days, nights, and seasons. For ancient peoples, the familiar and predictable cycles of nature became a way of organizing the unfamiliar and unpredictable happenings in the human world.

Religious myths, legends, and fables preserved in oral traditions satisfied the need of ancient people to know about their origins and predecessors. These tales often posited the existence of a golden age, during which the people lived harmoniously among themselves and with nature. The story in the Book of Genesis about Adam and Eve in the Garden of Eden provides an example. Other accounts presumed a close relationship with supernatural beings in which the gods and goddesses possessed humanlike characteristics and achieved their purposes through the manipulation and control of the lesser beings. In Greek mythology, the deities competed with one another for love and power, waged war on one another, and sometimes experienced failure. Infallibility was not necessarily an attribute of supernatural beings in the ancient world. The gods and goddesses also displayed a capacity for cruelty when they sought vengeance and inflicted retribution. When disasters and cataclysms took place, ancient people normally attributed them to the will of supernatural powers. The Greek notion of hubris, meaning self-destructive pride, required that the gods bring down mere mortals who overreached themselves. In all likelihood, such myths and legends also had political importance. By affirming a connection with the divinities through lineage or proximity, ancient rulers could legitimate their right to govern.

Some ancient peoples kept no records and hence have no recoverable history, except memories enshrined in oral traditions. Others, such as the Egyptians, Sumerians, Assyrians, and Hittites, left written artifacts dating from the third and second millennia BCE. Many of these consisted of lists and inscriptions recounting the deeds of great men. They testified to the emergence of a primitive historical consciousness, perhaps a sense of chronology, but showed little appreciation for the effect of one event upon another or the interrelationships among them. Instead, these registers presented bits of information in isolation from others. Sometimes they recited the major accomplishments or occurrences during the reign of a king, noting the year the wall was built or the temple completed, the time of the great famine or plague, or when enemies laid waste to the city. Accounts of warfare figured prominently. Graphic, brutal, even sadistic, descriptions reported terrible punishments visited upon conquered foes. An Assyrian document reported these acts performed by King Assurnâsirpal:

> 600 of their warriors I put to the sword; 3,000 captives I burned with fire; I did not leave a single one of them alive to serve as a hostage . . . Hulai, their governor, I flayed and his skin I spread upon the wall of the city; the city I destroyed, I devastated, I burned with fire.[1]

In another episode, the same monarch cut off the hands, noses, and ears of another set of adversaries, put out their eyes, and removed their heads with which he constructed a pillar. Such documents contained the raw material of history but did not in themselves constitute history. They provided no interpretation or analysis. They reported victories in battle but not the means of winning. The blood lust exhibited in them suggests why the horror of recollecting the past might have repelled ancient peoples.

The Jews of ancient Israel developed a different outlook. For them, history became more important than for any other ancient people. Indeed, it became a kind of obsession, the comprehension of which established the meaning of their existence and affirmed their own unique sense of destiny. Through the processes of history, the ancient Hebrews forged a distinctive relationship with their God, Yahweh. He had chosen them as a special people with particular obligations and responsibilities. The experience of deliverance from bondage in Egypt into the Promised Land became a memory seared upon the Jewish consciousness. In return, they had a commitment to comport themselves according to the law. By their conception of the covenant, the Jewish people would enjoy peace and plenty as long as they complied with the divine will. In contrast, calamity, suffering, and woe would descend upon them if they violated the Ten Commandments. The Jews saw the hand of God in human affairs. He rewarded good and faithful behavior and punished transgressions. The Jews reported their history accordingly in the books of the Old Testament.

Hebrew historical writing drew more on religious experience and faith than on critical or rational inquiry. The Jews interpreted the events in the lives of their people according to intense convictions. Bias and inconsistency crept into their narratives. Jewish writers occasionally incorporated different versions of the same events from diverse oral traditions. Nevertheless, they also displayed a capacity for hardheaded realism and objectivity. A remarkable passage in the Second Book of Samuel describes the antics of King David at a festival, "leaping and dancing" about while uncovering himself before a group of handmaidens. Much disturbed by the scene, Michal, the daughter of Saul, disdained David and later, upon encountering him, remarked ironically, "How glorious was the king of Israel today." As observed by Michael Grant, a historian of the ancient world, "David does not show up very brilliantly there."[2] In spite of his heroic stature, he was depicted unidealistically. The Jews knew how to exercise some measure of detachment.

The Greeks contributed something of immense significance to the development of historical thinking. They invented critical history as a method of sorting out the true from the false. In the classical Greek language, the term *histor* referred to a learned man who settled legal disputes. While making inquiries, he looked into the facts and determined their accuracy. Subsequently, as Michael Grant explains, the word *historie* meant "a search for the rational explanation and understanding of phenomena." In the fifth century BC, two geniuses, Herodotus and Thucydides, brought about an intellectual revolution by employing rational techniques and creating the writing of history.

The Greeks initially depicted the past as moving in a cycle and cast it in heroic epic poems such as Homer's *The Iliad* and *The Odyssey*. These grand, noble tales, drawn from oral traditions, were not history, even though the Greeks may have thought of them as such. Rather, they consisted of legends, myths, and fables in which gods, goddesses, and humans acted together, and supernatural forces often accounted for the progression of events. Divine will figured prominently in human affairs. Before history could exist, a test of reason had to take place. The great accomplishments of Herodotus and Thucydides provided a model for all subsequent written history. Many modern scholars still regard the two men as ranking among the greatest historians of all time. Historiography, that is, the history of historical writing, still holds them in high esteem. Indeed, new editions based on more readable translations have recently appeared, obtaining critical acclaim from scholars and indicating an ongoing interest. These writings took the form of prose, not poetry, and allowed each author to indulge a talent in storytelling before live audiences.[3]

The Histories by Herodotus of Halicarnassus told of the Greek wars against Persia during the third decade of the fifth century BCE. The first portion provided historical background while exploring the origin of the quarrel between the two contestants. The remainder recounted the details of Persian expeditions against Greece under the kings Darius and Xerxes. Scholars do not know much about Herodotus's life. Presumably, he lived about a generation after these events, and he traveled widely in order to collect material. The Persian Wars impressed him as the most important events in world history, and he made them the framework of his narrative. As he explained, he had two purposes in mind: "to preserve the memory of the past by putting on record the astonishing achievements both of our own and of the Asiatic peoples" and "to show how the two races came into conflict."[4] He achieved these aims and much more. Frequent digressions in the narrative dispensed an array of fascinating information, providing among other things a means of entertainment for his audience. His ethnographic and geographic accounts also suggested a broadly cultural approach. Herodotus wanted to know why the Nile flooded each year and who built the Pyramids. Many things piqued his curiosity, and intriguing observations followed. The Babylonians lacked medical doctors and developed a practice of putting invalids in the street where they could receive advice from passersby, and the Persians had a habit of deliberating twice on important issues, once while drunk and once while sober. Conclusions reached in one condition served as a check on the other.

Herodotus not only liked to tell a good story but also employed rigorous methods. He checked his information against the reports of eyewitnesses and participants and also consulted the documents available to him—inscriptional records, archives, and official chronicles. He also relied less on the custom of explaining events in the human world as the outcome of divine will. To be sure, he never succeeded in rendering a completely secular account of history. The deities still had a role to play. But Herodotus, more than any predecessor, interpreted the course of human affairs as the product of human will.

Thucydides, an Athenian, wrote *The Peloponnesian War*, an account of the struggle between Athens and Sparta during the last three decades of the fifth century BC. Thucydides took part in the conflict as a military commander and suffered the effects of the great plague in Athens, a horror vividly described in his writing. When forced into exile by the humiliation of a military defeat, he spent the next twenty years gathering materials for his work. Like Herodotus, he picked warfare as his subject. As he explained, he began his history "at the very outbreak of the war, in the belief that it was going to be a great war and more worth writing about than any of those which had happened in the past." He also wanted his history to be useful. Expressing a belief typical of his time, he affirmed a cyclical view in the expectation that "what happened in the past . . . will, in due course, tend to be repeated with some degree of similarity."[5] Thucydides intended his writing to have instructional importance as a guide to action in the future. Although history would never repeat itself exactly, he anticipated the development of parallel circumstances and believed that the consciousness of history would bestow many benefits. All leaders should learn from the mistakes of the past. Indeed, they could master the arts of politics, statecraft, and warfare only from the study of history.

Thucydides employed scrupulous methods. As a careful student of causation, he identified the process by which the Peloponnesian War came about. His analysis attributed the war's real or underlying reason to Sparta's fear of Athens's growing power. He also paid heed to individual motives but used a convention sometimes troublesome for modern scholars. Following the practices of Greek drama and Herodotus, Thucydides had historical figures deliver speeches in which they revealed their aims and intentions. Critics have attacked the use of such monologues as false. Even if the historian actually had heard them, how could he remember all the details? Apologists, in contrast, have pointed out that while not literally true, such devices enabled Thucydides to elucidate his understanding of the character, motives, and goals of the actor. In a sense, Thucydides had them say what their nature and the situation called for.

Thucydides, more than Herodotus, explained events in secular terms. In *The Peloponnesian War*, things happened not because the gods willed them but because of human activities. People had to endure the consequences of their own acts. Thucydides also strove for objectivity. His detachment and single-minded determination to stick to the essentials of the story made for less entertainment than Herodotus. No amusing digressions provided diversions for the listener or the reader. But the undoubted brilliance of his work inspired David Hume many centuries later to write, "The first page of Thucydides is the beginning of all true history."[6]

The quality of Greek historical writing declined after Herodotus and Thucydides. Much also became lost to posterity. Nevertheless, the two masters exerted strong influence over their scholarly progeny. In the second century BCE, Polybius, a Greek, embraced them as his models. He insisted that a historian must travel to see the sites, participate in public events, and utilize the documentary records. He must also have a grand theme. Polybius's *Universal History* told of Rome's expansion over the whole of the Mediterranean world. He also intended that his work have useful effects. As a form of practical instruction, it should equip serious readers to better act upon the future. Polybius passed on to the Romans the best of the Greek traditions in historical writing.

The Romans, strongly affected by the Greeks, also concentrated their attention on the political and military activities of the ruling elites. But, unlike the Greeks, they displayed less concern for detachment and objectivity. As serious moralists, they preferred to pass judgment and depict what they regarded as blameworthy or exemplary. Late in the first century BCE, for example, Sallust wrote from an outsider's point of view about the affairs of state, taking the leaders to task for their corruption and misdeeds and warning of the effects of decadence and decay. Titus Livy reported on the reign of Augustus, a period of 45 years during which peace returned after an era of conflict and civil war. His *History of Rome*, comprising an astounding 142 volumes, emphasized the role of civic virtue in the expansion of the Roman Republic. Unlike the historians who also performed as men of action, such as Thucydides, Titus Livy never held a public office, instead devoting his whole life to research and writing. The Romans also developed an interest in biography, emphasizing the role of personal character. Among the most famous biographers, Plutarch, writing in Greek, studied the roles of soldiers and statesmen, and Suetonius composed *Lives of the Caesars*.

Two Romans, Julius Caesar and Cornelius Tacitus, took on special significance. Caesar's *Commentaries* recounted firsthand his military exploits against the Gauls, Germans, and Britons in the middle of the first century BCE. This uniquely original work, spare and unadorned, established a stylistic model of Latin prose and also a new literary genre. As the memoirs of a field commander, Caesar's writings showed less interest in character and personality than in action. As a result, scholars had more information about the Gallic War than about any other military operation in the ancient world. Caesar also wrote with an eye on his reputation before the governing classes in Rome and before posterity. Political and military memoirs are seldom self-effacing.

Tacitus, Rome's greatest historian, produced several works on political and military subjects. The most notable, *The Annals of Imperial Rome*, described imperial affairs from the beginning of Tiberius's reign in 14 CE until the year 68, soon after the death of Nero. Written early in the second century CE, the book depicted personalities and also the corruption and degeneracy of Rome's rulers. Typical of Roman historians, Tacitus, formerly a state official, commended public virtue and condemned immorality, especially the personal excesses of the emperors and the self-serving cliques around them. He called them to account, often with sardonic irony and deep pessimism. Tacitus put scant faith in the redemptive capabilities of human nature. For him, Rome, the center of the world, had gone into decline. His main themes addressed the growth of political tyranny and the collapse of Roman virtue. While employing the traditional format, a narration of events year by year, he emphasized the dangers of concentrating political power in one man, always a hazardous practice because it allows individual character flaws to inflict maximum damage. Tacitus's tales of wrongdoing in the struggle for personal advancement featured adultery, incest, murder, matricide, patricide, and infanticide. He shared with Lord Acton a view expressed some eighteen centuries later that "power tends to corrupt, and absolute power corrupts absolutely." The careers of the debauched Tiberius and the brutal Nero provided cases in point.

Meanwhile, an emerging Christian view of history took on more cosmopolitan forms, extending beyond the provincial and self-centered fixations of Greece and Rome. It developed slowly during several centuries and out of harsh experience. The earliest Christians never developed much historical consciousness. They conceived of themselves as living in a small, closed universe, very near the termination of time. Because the end of the world and the Second Coming of Christ dominated their expectations, their anticipation of the future held more significance than their perception of the past. Later, when they had to face up to the fact that their religious prophecies had not come true, they could not avoid a confrontation with history.

For one reason, when Christian missionaries sought converts in the world of the Gentiles, they needed to establish the authority of revealed religion based on its historicity. From various sources, such as oral traditions and the like, they compiled the Gospels, consisting of stories about the life and sayings of Jesus and his ministry, crucifixion, and resurrection. The Christian insistence that such occurrences actually had taken place grounded their beliefs in an interpretation of historical experience and affirmed the veracity of their claims before believers. History also became important when the early Christians tried to devise proper connections with the Old Testament. The identification of Jesus with the Messiah of Hebrew prophecy necessarily engaged them with the teachings of the Hebrew prophets. Once the early Christians came to regard the Old Testament as Holy Scripture, they also formulated an explanation of the relationship between the past, the present, and the future. Ultimately they conceived the whole of the Old Testament as an anticipation of Jesus Christ and a preparation for him. For them, such prophecies became an important means by which to ascertain the designs of Divine Providence.

Christianity later took on some of the attributes of universal history through its efforts to appeal to pagans. To obtain prestige within the Roman Empire, again arguing on the basis of history, Christians tried to show that Hebrew wisdom had roots more ancient than Greek philosophy. Moses after all lived a long time before Plato. Other attempts to link the experiences of Jews and Gentiles compelled Christians to develop ideas about the secular history of humankind. The very nature of the Scriptures, of course, contributed by starting with the Creation and then telling about the beginnings of humankind and its subsequent division into distinctive groups. Indeed, Christian writers of universal history followed this convention until the eighteenth and nineteenth centuries, typically by beginning their narratives with creation accounts based on their understanding of the Book of Genesis.

Christians within the Roman Empire suffered the effects of oppression and persecution for their beliefs but obtained a great triumph when the Emperor Constantine converted to their religion early in the fourth century. This outcome encouraged the writing of ecclesiastical history, detailing the rise of Christianity throughout the Mediterranean world. Eusebius of Caesarea in Syria Palestine was an early practitioner. His *History of the Church* and other works demonstrated how all previous history, especially the Hebrew experience, had led to the Christian revelation. Eusebius took pains to rebut the pagan charge that the newly invented Christian religion appealed only to ignorant people. Quite the contrary, he argued, the traditions stretched backward in time to a glorious past far beyond the Greeks. His work celebrated the Christian victory in taking possession of Rome.

A century later under very different circumstances, St. Augustine, the bishop of Hippo in North Africa, wrote *The City of God*, the most influential Christian interpretation of history ever devised. Augustine devised his work as a response to a catastrophe in the year 410, when Alaric and the Goths captured the city of Rome and perpetrated three days of looting, pillage, and rape. This horrifying event, verging on the unimaginable, ignited fears of resurgent barbarism overwhelming Roman civilization and also provoked pagan charges of Christian responsibility. Adherents of the new religion supposedly had led the people away from the ancient Roman gods, who in this way had taken retribution upon the Eternal City for its neglect. Augustine in reply wrote his powerful work between the years 413 and 426. To an extent he labored as a partisan and polemicist in defense of the Christians. In the first ten chapters, he absolved them of the blame, showing that equivalent disasters had occurred before, even when the inhabitants worshiped pagan gods. In the remaining ten chapters, he developed a new and unique approach to universal history. Drawing upon earlier Jewish and Christian writings, he developed an analysis that would dominate European thinking for over a 1,000 years.

As an organizing principle, Augustine established a dualism that made a fundamental distinction between the profane and the sacred. He referred to the former as the earthly "city of man" and the latter as the heavenly "city of God." Though intermingled on Earth for the remainder of time, the two communities took on different characteristics. The first, the secular city, featured self-love and resulted in absorption with the ways of the flesh. The second, the Eternal City, affirmed spiritual love for God above all things. Although Augustine traced the progress of both cities until his own time, his main preoccupation concerned sacred history, that is, his attempt to elucidate the ways of God and correlate human events with biblical accounts.

Augustine's work also held important implications for the philosophy of history. His sense of time, derived from Hebrew conceptions, rejected outright the Greek idea of cyclical movements. For Augustine, endless revolvings and pointless repetitions would have rendered history meaningless, in effect nullifying divine influence and purpose. Rather, he thought of history as moving along a line with a clear beginning marked by the Creation, a middle, and an end. The birth and death of Christ denoted the central events, and the salvation of all believers at the termination of time signified the completion of the process. The concluding triumph of the city of God over the city of man would result in the fulfillment of the final aim, the transcendence of believers beyond history into the realm of the eternal.

Augustine's convictions, endorsed in high forms of art, literature, and music by masters such as Michelangelo, Dante, and Handel, made a profound imprint upon Western civilization. The schema characterized by the two cities and the movement of events along a line inspired Christian writers throughout the medieval period and after. They attributed prime significance to teleology and eschatology, that is, to those branches of philosophy and theology concerned with the nature of providential design and the conclusion of time during the last days. Christian predictions about the end of this world took on an Augustinian understanding of God's plan by which the Divinity sought to work out his will through history.

For over ten centuries, writers on historical subjects during the Middle Ages labored under Augustine's influence. Though Europeans during this time made distinctions between secular and sacred history, they paid more attention to the latter and composed ecclesiastical, or church, histories designed to delineate the progress of God's work in this world. Characteristically, the writing took the form of annals and chronicles set forth by priests and monks. Such accounts became stylized based on Augustine's model. Normally they contained a summary of universal history since the Creation, influenced often by Old Testament accounts, an affirmation of God's purpose and will, and then statements of occurrences in recent times, showing the immanence of the divine presence in reality.

The annals, the more rudimentary form, set forth lists in brief-entry form that recorded memorable events in a locality during a single year, making a kind of yearbook or register. An aggregation of such entries arranged in an annual sequence with some additional narrative produced a chronicle. Though usually intended to record God's activities and manifestations, such sources also contained information about secular life in Christian communities. The compilers told about the goings-on within the monastery, the deaths of bishops and kings, the outcomes of battles, and the construction of new churches. They also reported on unusual episodes, often taken as omens or portents that would help foretell the future. Eclipses and floods, the appearance of strange animals, or the birth of malformed children provided occasions for uncertainty and wonderment.

Though annals and chronicles became the main vehicles for historical writing during the medieval period, the priests and monks usually assembled their records in anonymity and hence posed a problem for modern scholars who seek to identify them. Some carried out their labors for personal reasons, others to keep an official record for some kind of patron, possibly commissioned by a royal court. The problem of determining authorship became even more difficult because of the prevailing practice, sometimes over several generations, of circulating the documents from one monastery to another for emendations and exchanges of information.

Although often the work of several authors, the annals and chronicles bore some uniform characteristics. For example, they testified to a widespread belief in Divine Providence. For medieval writers, one God with paternal authority indisputably stood above humanity, watched over the course of events, and influenced them through divine intervention. Such expressions of faith influenced the discussions of human behavior and the analyses of phenomena. The compilers of annals and chronicles looked upon religion as the ultimate concern of humankind and believed that history moved teleologically according to design toward a foreordained conclusion directed by God.

Such proclivities produced a tendency toward moralistic examinations of human experience. Medieval writing often rendered verdicts and judgments, thus raising questions in the present about objectivity and truthfulness. Contemporary scholars have recognized the issue as a modern one. Most medieval chronicles would not have seen it as a problem. The intention of telling the truth was what mattered. Procopius, for example, declared that "truth alone is appropriate to history," and Matthew Paris invoked an even stronger sanction against untruthful historians: "If they commit to writing that which is false, they are not acceptable to the Lord." To assure credibility, medieval writers usually informed readers of their sources of information. The following examples suggest some additional characteristics.

Procopius, a Byzantine of the sixth century, composed contemporary histories of the wars of Emperor Justinian I against the Ostrogoths, Vandals, Visigoths, and Persians. His major work is known as *History of the Wars*. As a writer well versed in classical Greek historiography, he embraced as his models the works of Herodotus, Thucydides, and Polybius. He also emulated their methods. He used his political connections to good advantage and managed to accompany generals onto the battlefield. Probably he also gained access to state papers and official archives. Procopius merits a high place in the ranks of medieval historians because of the quality and persuasiveness of his writing. Nevertheless, modern authorities concede that they have no way to test his trustworthiness because no other sources exist against which to measure his accounts.

The Venerable Bede engaged in a very different kind of scholarship early in the eighth century. He spent his life in the monastery at Jarrow in Northumbria in the north of England studying, teaching, and writing on religious, educational, and historical subjects. One of the great centers of learning in its day, his location featured an excellent library. Modern scholars acclaim Bede as one of the most learned men of the early Middle Ages. His *Ecclesiastical History of the English People* is the first reliable description of early Britain, taking into account both sacred and secular aspects. Bede initially became interested in history while pondering the problem of how to establish an accurate chronology of events and the proper dates for Christian festivals. Later he became intrigued with the arrival of Christianity in England, the expansion of the Church throughout the country, and its effects on cultural and intellectual life. He discussed extensively the literary activities of monks. Though Bede seldom conducted research in the archives and repositories of the great churches and abbeys and never participated in battles, he had a high regard for valid sources and often arranged to have written accounts and other narratives brought to him from Canterbury.

In the twelfth century, Otto of Freising emerged as the greatest of the German chroniclers. Born into a noble family, a nephew of

Emperor Frederick I Barbarossa, Otto became the bishop of Freising, near Salzburg in Austria, and stayed there all his life. He wrote two important works: *The Deeds of Emperor Frederick Barbarossa*, a laudatory political biography of his uncle, and the *Chronicle or History of the Two Cities*, a universal history modeled on the work of St. Augustine. Otto of Freising employed a linear conception of history and presumed the existence of a beginning, in the Creation, and an end, in the Second Coming, after which Christians would enjoy everlasting bliss in eternity. He vividly presented the notion of the two cities and took it more literally than St. Augustine, seeing the Church as the actual representative of the Holy City. Yet as a member of the royal family and a close observer of imperial affairs, he was more conciliatory in his attitude toward the secular state. He possessed little faith that Christianity could moderate the baser aspects of human nature in this world.

Two chroniclers of the late medieval period, Matthew Paris and Jean Froissart, also merit mention. Matthew Paris, an English monk in the thirteenth century, recorded the affairs of church and state in his own time. His *Greater Chronicle* incorporated an edited version of *Flowers of History*, the work of a predecessor, Roger of Wendover, but Matthew's narrative upon reaching the year 1236 became an independent and original source. Broader in scope than much medieval writing, it described events in England and elsewhere, including Western Europe, the Papal states, the Latin Empire of Constantinople, the Holy Land, and even Russia. Matthew paid special heed to politics and international intrigue but also liked to remind his readers of God's presence in this world, the role of Divine Providence, and the impending realities of death and last judgment. As with much medieval historical writing, according to God's plan, divine punishment almost always followed the enactment of a sin.

In the fourteenth century, the *Chronicles* of Jean Froissart, a French priest, also centered on political and military affairs of state. Froissart wrote with self-conscious detachment and endeavored to tell the truth in an age of chivalry. He stirringly depicted battles and heroic deeds by knights in combat. He also assumed that the divine played a role in human affairs but worked hard to obtain accurate information. As a historian mainly concerned with the aristocracy, he took little interest in the mundane lives of the lower classes.

In an illuminating work entitled *The Past as Text: The Theory and Practice of Medieval Historiography*, Gabrielle M. Spiegel presents a series of essays in which she examines various aspects of French historical writing and makes an important point: medieval historiography possessed a large measure of political utility. As Spiegel explains, "Like law, historiography played an important role in the politics of a traditional society dependent, as was medieval society, upon the past for legitimacy." Indeed, she claims, "Surely few complex societies have so clearly regulated their life in accordance with their vision of history." Custom, that is, historical precedent, wielded a governing influence over politics and society and provided a means of justifying the status quo as consistent with the will of God.[7]

In summary, the historiographical traditions of the medieval period modified the Greek approach by putting supernatural power back into history. This tendency persisted well into the modern era. By the fourteenth century, such writings had become formalistic and repetitive. Medieval chroniclers typically concentrated upon affairs in their own time and relied on earlier authorities for information about previous ages. By and large, they lacked the intellectual and methodological means to employ original sources and to recover their meaning and significance. Instead, they depended on the veracity of their predecessors. For this reason, history as a body of knowledge had little standing in medieval universities. No one could demonstrate with any reliability the truthfulness and believability of historical assertions. Subsequently, important changes took place between the fourteenth and nineteenth centuries. During those 500 years of turmoil and upheaval, history achieved the status of an academic discipline and obtained a new capacity to verify its principal claims.

RECOMMENDED READINGS

Historians at Work, Vol. 1: *From Herodotus to Froissart*, eds Peter Gay and Gerald J. Cavanaugh (New York: Harper and Row, 1972), provides a convenient anthology of the writings of the great historians in the ancient and medieval worlds. *The Ancient Historians* by Michael Grant (New York: Charles Scribner's Sons, 1970) considers the Greeks and the Romans. New, more readable editions appear in Herodotus, *The Histories*, translated by Robin Waterfield (New York: Oxford University Press, 1998), and *The Landmark Thucydides: A Comprehensive Guide to the Peloponnesian War*, translated by Robert B. Strassler (New York: Free Press, 1996). Herbert Butterfield, *The Origins of History* (New York: Basic Books, 1981), describes the inception of historical thinking and Christian renditions. Contributions in the medieval period are considered in Joseph Dahmus's, *Seven Medieval Historians* (Chicago: Nelson-Hall, 1982); and Indrikis Sterns's, *The Greater Medieval Historians: An Interpretation and a Bibliography* (Washington: University Press of America, 1981). John Barker's, *The Superhistorians: Makers of Our Past* (New York: Charles Scribner's Sons, 1982) contains fine essays on Herodotus, Thucydides, and St. Augustine. A sophisticated and detailed study by Ernst Breisach, *Historiography: Ancient, Medieval, and Modern*, 2nd ed. (Chicago: University of Chicago Press, 1994), covers in much greater depth many of the issues under consideration here. John Gould's volume *Herodotus* (New York: St. Martin's Press, 1989), in a new series devoted to great historians, provides an introduction for modern readers. Ronald Mellor's, *Tacitus* (New York: Routledge, 1993) does the same. Denys Hay, *Annalists and Historians: Western Historiography from the Eighth to the Eighteenth Centuries* (London: Methuen and Co., 1977), presents an overview. *Versions of History from Antiquity to the Enlightenment*, edited by Donald R. Kelley (New Haven: Yale University Press, 1991), contains excerpts from many of the most prominent historians. Kelley's later volume, *Faces of History: Historical Inquiry from Herodotus to Herder* (New Haven: Yale University Press, 1998), provides a critical survey and interpretation. Part I, "Beginnings—East and West," and part II, "The Medieval World," in the *Companion to Historiography* (New York: Routledge, 1997), edited by Michael Bentley, have much utility. Another volume by Chris Given-Wilson, *Chronicles: The Writing of History in Medieval England* (New York: Hambleton and London, 2004), includes many insights. Gabrielle M. Spiegel's, *The Past as Text: The Theory and Practice of Medieval Historiography* (Baltimore: Johns Hopkins University Press, 1997) contains a set of illuminating and suggestive essays. Finally, all readers with an interest in historiography will find indispensable John Burrow's iconoclastic book, *A History of Histories: Epics, Chronicles, Romances and Inquiries from Herodotus and Thucydides to the Twentieth Century* (New York: Alfred A. Knopf, 2008).

ENDNOTES

1. Quoted in Herbert Butterfield, *The Origins of History* (New York: Basic Books, 1981), 76–77.
2. Michael Grant, *The Ancient Historians* (New York: Charles Scribner's Sons, 1970), 10–11.
3. Herodotus, *The Histories*, trans. Robin Waterfield (New York: Oxford University Press, 1998); Robert B. Strassler, ed., *The Landmark Thucydides: A Comprehensive Guide to the Peloponnesian War* (New York: Free Press, 1996).

3

HISTORICAL CONSCIOUSNESS IN THE MODERN AGE

A modern historical consciousness among Europeans developed gradually over the course of several centuries in the years after the Renaissance. Fundamentally, the change entailed a transformation away from supernatural explanations and toward secular approaches while studying the past. Methodological constraints compelled such a shift. As historians eventually realized, it was one thing to say that God acted in history and another to determine where and when. History as a professional discipline acquired a more scientific outlook as methods of research, criticism, analysis, and interpretation became more rigorous and as practitioners tried to keep abreast of stunning advances in other areas of human knowledge. A splendid, detailed, up-to-date examination of the process appears in John Burrow's *A History of Histories: Epics, Chronicles, Romances and Inquiries from Herodotus and Thucydides to the Twentieth Century* (2008).

In modern times, historians, much as scholars in other academic areas, abandoned attempts to determine ultimate or final causes, that is, God's role in the historical and natural worlds. Religious teleology for the most part fell into disuse. No modern scholar working in a reputable field can claim legitimately to possess the means by which to verify any statements about the role of divine influences in history and nature. As manifestations of faith, statements about God's purposes are not subject to proof by reason, logic, and evidence. Rather, they occupy a position in a different category of discourse. Consequently, historians as historians cannot with any veracity address such matters and must concentrate their efforts on devising methods by which to expand their understanding of the knowable world.

To this end, historians have sought ways of enlarging in the present our comprehension of all kinds of artifacts from the past. In this way, they attempted to recapture the spirit of the Greeks by approaching the study of history critically and putting more demands upon the evidence than upon traditions of faith and authority. The transformation took place incrementally over a long period of time, beginning with the resurgence of interest in the ancient world during the Renaissance, then later reacting to religious, scientific, and philosophical currents, and culminating with the establishment of university-based historical studies in the nineteenth century. During this formative period, Leopold von Ranke and other scholars changed the practice of history into a profession and laid down the main directions of development until the present day.

One of the first intimations of an impending break with medieval historiography occurred during the early stages of the Renaissance in the fourteenth century. The life labors of Francesco Petrarca, usually anglicized as Petrarch, aimed at the recovery of the traditions of ancient Rome. A native of the city of Florence in Italy, Petrarch devoted his attention to the preservation and transcription of classical writings. For him, the Roman experience incorporated the best attributes of humankind. "What else, then," he asked, "is all history, if not the praise of Rome?" Though concerned primarily with the collection of literary artifacts, he also wrote a history of Rome, *Lives of Illustrious Men*, and contributed to the establishment of a new, secular interpretation of history, but he did so without directly attacking Christian authority. His search for Rome set forth an alternative vision of human beings and their world in which real events had more than just symbolic importance. The actuality of human striving and attainment for him held great allure.

In the sixteenth century, another Florentine, Niccolò Machiavelli, focused attention on the human dimension in history through his writings on politics. Born in 1469, the son of a lawyer, Machiavelli received an education that included reading the Latin and Italian classics. In 1494, he was embarking on a political career when the combined effects of a French invasion and Girolamo Savonarola's religious uprising resulted in the ouster of Lorenzo the Magnificent, the ruler of Florence and a member of the house of Medici. Machiavelli subsequently served the Florentine republic in various capacities until the restoration of the Medicis in 1512. Forced into exile on a farm outside of the city, Machiavelli then spent his time trying to regain his lost influence and writing about the conduct of politics, the true description of which became his obsession. His famous work, *The Prince*, set forth a body of precepts showing that the actual methods of governance had scant connection with medieval political theory. According to this handbook on the uses of political power, the wise prince had to know when to employ duplicitous or cynical means. Power and the proper utilization of it to achieve personal advantage formed his great theme. History for Machiavelli turned into a kind of potpourri of examples by which to illustrate his maxims. His *History of Florence* detailed the intrigue and machinations characteristic of politics in his own city and depicted human behavior as motivated by opportunism and aggrandizement.

The rediscovered wisdom of the Greeks and Romans inspired the Italians during the Renaissance and provided models, especially the writings of Thucydides, Polybius, and Titus Livy. Following such leads, Italian historians often dwelt on things political and military. Machiavelli's younger contemporary, Francesco Guicciardini, adhered to classical themes in his *History of Italy*. A better historian than Machiavelli, Guicciardini carried out more research, notably in the papal archives, understood more subtly the diversity of human nature, and espoused a less provincial outlook. He examined the history of a larger geographic area, strove to provide a broad, interpretive framework, and showed some of the connecting features in various aspects of Italian experience.

Although such historians addressed modern problems, various methodological shortcomings still impeded the development of a modern historical consciousness. Scholars had not yet developed appropriate techniques for elucidating the meaning of historical artifacts within the context of their own times, places, and cultures. To be sure, antiquarians and humanists during the Renaissance collected and preserved Greek and Roman documents and by so doing inadvertently created repositories of immense value for future historians. But they took more interest in venerating the memory and emulating the style of the ancients than in subjecting them to analysis and interpretation. Philology, that is, the science of verifying and authenticating old manuscripts—now called hermeneutics—preoccupied them more than history. In this endeavor, they developed critical techniques that made possible the identification of forgeries, alterations, and mistaken transcription.

A famous example involved a political fraud. According to a widely accepted myth in the late Middle Ages, Constantine the Great, the first Christian emperor of Rome, upon his conversion to the faith had bestowed religious and political authority over the Roman Empire in the West on the bishop of Rome, in this case Pope Sylvester II. The popes in later years had invoked the legend as a basis for establishing their claims to power. In 1440, Lorenzo Valla proved the story false in a brilliant piece of detective work entitled *Discourse on the Forgery of the Alleged Donation of Constantine.* Using the methodologies of textual criticism, or philology, Valla demonstrated that the presumed substantiating document abounded with errors, inconsistencies, and anachronisms, showing that no one could have written the *Discourse* in the fourth century. The faked document had to have come from a later time.

The Protestant Reformation and the ensuing religious and political upheavals in the sixteenth and seventeenth centuries in Europe intensified the interest in history among the warring factions, often becoming a tool of partisans in polemical debates. Antagonists on all sides invoked the past to give authority to their positions in the present. The issues centered on the role of the Church in interpreting the word of God to believers, the character of the Bible as a historical text, and the circumstances surrounding the development of Christianity as an institutional religion.

Protestants attacked their adversaries by insisting that papal control had corrupted the purity of belief and practice inherited from the early Church. In Germany, Martin Luther and Philip Melanchthon used history as a means for challenging Roman Catholic traditions. Another group of Lutheran scholars under Matthias Flacius Illyricus later published a study of thirteen volumes entitled *Magdeburg Centuries* to document Protestant assertions that the Roman hierarchy had distorted and perverted the teachings of Christ and the apostles. Similarly, Robert Barnes, an Englishman, wrote *Lives of Roman Pontiffs*, in which he ascribed an assortment of misdeeds and wrongdoings to high Church officials. Roman Catholics fought back, using history in defense of their beliefs and practices. In 1571, a papal commission chose Caesar Boronius to rebut the *Magdeburg Centuries.* According to his *Ecclesiastical Annals*, the various post-apostolic changes had legitimacy as clarifications and interpretations of Christ's teachings and, in addition, as manifestations of the workings of the Holy Spirit.

Such controversies divided Christendom and resulted in the establishment of the first professorships in history at European universities. The Lutherans established one at Heidelberg and the Calvinists another at Leyden. Although such innovations contributed to the dissemination of professional history, a more immediate effect accelerated the disintegration of uniform Christian interpretations of history and also a gap between sacred and secular forms of understanding. As a consequence of the Protestant Reformation, the consensus in support of St. Augustine's version of universal history ceased to exist, and no new, unifying approach emerged immediately as a replacement.

The great scientific revolutions of the seventeenth century raised other unsettling questions about the problem of devising reliable and accurate accounts of the past. Following the discoveries of Newton, Kepler, and Galileo, a scientific worldview took hold of European intellectuals, many of whom doubted the feasibility of obtaining verifiable knowledge in imprecise fields of investigation such as history. For philosophers schooled in the scientific method such as Descartes, Spinoza, and Leibnitz, mathematical formulations held the key to exactitude and certainty. As British historian B.A. Haddock observes, "Mathematics had removed the aura of mystery from nature, had freed enquiry from the obfuscation of medieval obscurantism, and it was thought that the same tool would be similarly successful in the study of man."

According to the champions of natural science, history as a discipline had failed in the development of verifiable methods. If historians could not express knowledge in conformance with mathematics, then they had either indulged in a "harmless but irrelevant enjoyment of confused perceptions" or embarked upon "a dangerous error in the path of truth." As Haddock notes, for the philosophers of natural science, "these mechanical methods were essentially timeless. They used a model of reason, eternally valid, based on their own mathematical procedures, which destroyed the validity of all other modes of experience."[1] They set before historians one of the great epistemological issues of the last four centuries, specifically, the degree to which the natural sciences can and should determine the forms of knowledge and understanding in the study of human affairs.

In spite of all the controversy over religion and philosophy, more pragmatically minded historians managed to produce enduring works. In 1566, Jean Bodin, a French teacher of jurisprudence, published *Methods for the Easy Comprehension of History*, in which he called for an expansion of legal studies as a means of escaping provincialism. He wanted to create a new kind of universal history comparing and contrasting the laws and customs of all nations. He employed complex categories, establishing distinctions among divine, natural, and human history and organizing the materials according to chronological and geographic criteria. He also insisted upon the preeminence of primary over secondary sources. A century later in 1681, another Frenchman, Jean Mabillon, published two volumes entitled *On Diplomatics*. Pronounced a masterpiece in the twentieth century by no less an authority than the great French medievalist Marc Bloch, this study demonstrated exacting scholarship while presenting the methods and techniques of deciphering ancient charters and manuscripts to determine their authenticity— a science known at the time as "diplomatics." The detection of forged documents had practical significance for historians and lawyers and could take on economic importance in disputes over land, property, and privilege. Through the use of comparative analysis, Mabillon proposed to identify error and inconsistency.

Such methodological tenacity was uncharacteristic of the seventeenth century. In the same year, Bishop Jacques Bénigne Bossuet's *Discourse on Universal History* appeared as a means of teaching morality to the Dauphin, the male heir of King Louis XIV. Thematically reminiscent of St. Augustine, the *Discourse* affirmed tradition and authority by employing a providential view and depicting the Roman Catholic Church as the chosen agent of God's will. A kind of throwback, this work recalled a style of writing from a time before the Reformation, the scientific revolution, and the methodologies of diplomatics.

The era of the Enlightenment produced a torrent of historical writing with significant effects on historical thinking. In the eighteenth century, European philosophers proclaimed the advent of a new age for humankind. Reason, rather than superstition, would guide human behavior. As a kind of corollary, the movement also implied a rebellion against the authority of traditional religion. In a famous and important book, *The Idea of History*, British philosopher and historian Robin G. Collingwood characterized the Enlightenment as an attempt "to secularize every department of human life and thought." He saw it as "a revolt not only against the power of institutional religion but against religion itself." As Collingwood explained, Voltaire, a leading figure, regarded himself as the advance agent in a crusade against Christianity and other backward, barbarous influences. His slogan "Ecrasez l'infâme" called upon his contemporaries to "crush the wicked thing."[2]

Meanwhile, competing tendencies appeared in the English-speaking world. An early attempt at critical history, William Camden's *Brittania*, published in 1586, focused on pre-Roman antiquity. It took on some of the attributes of later scholarship by depicting as false the heroic tales of King Arthur's time and also by espousing strong nationalism. According to one commentator, Camden "wanted to be both patriotic and scientific . . . an enormous assignment, but he succeeded magnificently."[3] Another Englishman, transplanted to North America, engaged in an impressive exercise in writing contemporary history. William Bradford began *Of Plymouth Plantation* in 1630 and continued it for two decades. This spare, simple narrative provided the most complete story of the Plymouth colony on Cape Cod in Massachusetts during the early years. Bradford served as governor for a long time. His stark tale of anguish and adversity recorded the trials endured by the settlers and incorporated a message regarded by all Protestant Pilgrims as true. The hand of God directed human history in inscrutable ways. Another example of writing contemporary history emerged from the great religious and political struggles in England between the Puritans and the Cavaliers in the middle of the seventeenth century. This subject over the years has preoccupied many students of English history as the nation's formative experience. An early account by Edward Hyde, the first Earl of Clarendon, entitled *History of the Rebellion and Civil Wars in England*, presented a passionate defense on behalf of the Church of England and the king against the assaults of tyranny, regicide, and irreligion.

Such issues produced deep divisions during the Enlightenment. The foremost historians—Voltaire, David Hume, and Edward Gibbon—disparaged the role of religion while depicting it as an impediment to human progress. For Voltaire, the priestly classes ranked among the great deceivers in all ages and places. Indeed, they functioned as the purveyors of bigotry, intolerance, and oppression. For Enlightenment historians, the liberation of people from religious superstition marked human advancement toward rationality and emancipation.

Attempts to move beyond the customary categories also typified the writing of history during the Enlightenment. Secular writing ordinarily comprised political and military affairs and centered on the activities of Western Europeans. Voltaire most notably extended the frontiers to encompass social, economic, and cultural dimensions and also non-Europeans. Indeed, he composed some of the first social and cultural history and developed a kind of fixation on the Chinese.

In spite of such laudable impulses, much of the written history during the Enlightenment suffered from a fundamental flaw: an incapacity to comprehend the behavior of historical actors on their own terms. The historians lacked a truly historical sense of development and context in the past. Locked into the precepts of their own time, they regarded their own values and aspirations as universal and absolute, the best toward which humankind could strive. Consequently, they regarded deviations in other times and other places as either aberration or folly.

Collingwood made the point pungently, arguing that "the historical outlook of the Enlightenment was not genuinely historical" at all. Rather, he described it as "polemical and antihistorical." Paradoxically, the past repelled historians, who interpreted it as a confining influence from which to escape. In Collingwood's words, historians regarded the past as "sheer error . . . a thing devoid of all positive value whatever." Accordingly, scholars had difficulty comprehending the past as the participants experienced it, and when gauged by the standards of the present, it failed to measure up. A related problem stemmed from a reluctance to carry out much archival research. Instead, historians preferred to draw on existing works. As Collingwood remarked, "They were not sufficiently interested in history for its own sake to persevere in the task of reconstructing the history of obscure and remote periods."[4]

Voltaire, the very embodiment of the Enlightenment spirit, personified the problem. The author of an immense number of works in many different literary genres, he also figured prominently in the development of historical writing. First and foremost, he insisted that history should have a practical purpose. Pursued reflectively and philosophically (*en philosophe*), the study of the past should contribute to the cause of Enlightenment by freeing readers from fallacy and misconception. Voltaire affirmed the point bluntly, claiming that "all ages resemble one another in respect of the criminal folly."[5] For the same reason, all merit historical study. Only by facing up to the shortcomings of the past could human beings achieve the necessary release. Voltaire intended further to write discriminating history, concentrating especially on "that which deserves the attention of all time, which paints the spirit and the customs of men, which may serve for instruction and to counsel the love of virtue, of the arts and of the fatherland."

Voltaire's principal historical works were *Philosophy of History*, later incorporated as an introduction into his *Essay on the Customs and the Spirit of Nations*, and his masterpiece, *The Age of Louis XIV*. In the first essay, employing in the title a term he coined, "philosophy of history," Voltaire intended to illuminate the mind of his mistress, Madame du Châtelet. By depicting philosophically the human advance out of barbarism, he showed the malignant influence of priests among the Egyptians, Hebrews, and Christians. In effect, he turned medieval historiography on its head. But Voltaire put little stock in basing claims on evidence. For him, reason and credibility, more than original documents, provided the test of truth. For example, he questioned the story of Noah's ark by asking "how many persons were in the ark to feed all the animals for ten whole months, and during the following year in which no food would be produced?" The second volume depicted the late seventeenth century, the age of Louis XIV, as one of four ages of "great attainment" in the history of humanity and hence an object of special attention. The other three ages took place in Greece under Pericles, in Rome under Caesar and Augustus, and in Constantinople after the fall of the city to Mahomet II. His portrait of the many achievements in Europe during the reign of Louis XIV amounted to the invention of cultural history.

Though less a polemicist than Voltaire, David Hume, a Scotsman, shared his secular bent. Contemporary critics denounced his philosophical works as the product of skepticism and atheism. In contrast, his historical works won for him fame and fortune. His six-volume *History of England* was one of the best and most popular in the eighteenth century. Moving backward in time, Hume wrote first about the Stuart kings, then the Tudors, and finally the invasion of Julius Caesar. Critical and iconoclastic in approach, Hume refused to put history in service to politics and wrecked romantic legends and patriotic myths. As a rigorous empiricist, he always hesitated to claim more than the observation of phenomena could warrant or to think that patterns of the past necessarily would recur in the future. Hume consequently found in history no particular sanction for any specific moral or legislative programs. Indeed, he mistrusted metaphysical claims and religious dogmatism as the breeders of fanaticism and instability. For him, the Puritan revolution against King Charles I served as a case in point. Political equipoise required an ability to adapt institutions to the dictates of experience.

Perhaps the greatest of the Enlightenment histories, *The Decline and Fall of the Roman Empire*, by Edward Gibbon, covered a period of 1,300 years from the first century until the Renaissance and ran to some million and a quarter words. Gibbon, an Englishman, spent twenty years of his life on the project but invested little effort in searching out new documents. Instead, he drew heavily on the works of seventeenth-century scholars and antiquarians. This colossal effort amounted to a synthesis of the existing research on the ancient and medieval worlds. It also transposed St. Augustine's thesis in *The City of God*. Rather than absolve Christians of responsibility for bringing about the terrible events leading to Rome's fall, Gibbon held them primarily accountable. To simplify his argument exceedingly, Gibbon maintained that the obsessions of a hard-pressed people with life after death resulted in the neglect of imperial interests and the need to maintain proper military defenses. Otherworldliness corroded the Roman will, undermined the Roman army, and brought about the collapse. In a kind of summary statement, Gibbon set forth the essentials of his view:

> The theologian may indulge the pleasing task of describing Religion as she descended from Heaven, arrayed in her native purity. A more melancholy duty is imposed on the historian. He must discover the inevitable mixture of error and corruption which she contracts in a long residence upon earth, among a weak and degenerate race of beings.[6]

This kind of condescension toward the past raised important methodological questions. Critics such as Robin G. Collingwood in the twentieth century attacked Enlightenment historians on the grounds that their insensitivity in effect violated the integrity of history. More specifically, they failed to empathize properly with the historical actors or comprehend their behavior accurately on their own terms. Rather, Enlightenment scholars indulged in exposés, reviling the past to obliterate and overcome it. Consequently, Collingwood denounced their writing as an enterprise gone fundamentally wrong. They had failed to carry out the historian's primary task, that is, to elucidate the past, not merely to condemn it. For Collingwood, the magnitude of irresponsibility took on even greater proportions because a methodological means for achieving the goal already existed. Giambattista Vico, an obscure Italian theorist from Naples, had shown the way.

Vico published his brilliant and innovative book in 1725. Hailed in the twentieth century as the product of genius, truly an anticipation of modern social science, *The New Science* had much less impact on the eighteenth century. In discouragement, Vico himself lamented of his work, "It has gone forth into a desert." No one initially paid much attention, even though Vico had provided the methodological means for resolving the dilemma of the Enlightenment historians. To overcome the confines of one's own time and to treat the past with a proper degree of historicity, he demonstrated that scholars had an obligation to reconstruct the mental universe of people in previous times in order to account for their actions. Voltaire could have learned a great deal from Vico.

Vico presented *The New Science* as a critical response to the overblown and exaggerated claims of natural science. For example, René Descartes had disenfranchised history as a branch of knowledge because of the notorious unreliability of traditional accounts, in his view a manifestation of fantasy and make-believe. Vico, in contrast, established an epistemology by which to set forth verifiable, true claims. While refraining from any denial of the validity of mathematics, he insisted upon the feasibility of other forms of knowing. To rebut Descartes' notion that the natural order constituted the most promising field for truthful inquiry, he insisted upon a kind of first principle. To understand anything fully, he argued, the observer must have made the thing under observation. Because God had created nature, only He could grasp the totality of it. In contrast, because human beings had made history, they possessed the capacity to arrive at a correct understanding, provided, of course, that they employed the right methods.

Vico conceived of history as a dynamic process of change characterized by a movement through three stages. Though admittedly Eurocentric in design, the scheme at least recognized that different people in different places and different times actually saw and experienced the world differently. As a devout Christian, Vico adhered to the essentials of the Old Testament rendition until the aftermath of the Great Flood but then put his own stamp on the course of events. Noah's descendants, after some 200 years of chaos, embarked upon a journey through the age of gods, the age of heroes, and the age of men. Vico believed that human nature underwent changes during the progression and that identifiable links connected beliefs and institutions into a whole. During the first stage, an age of sensation, ferocity and cruelty typified human nature, and governments took on theocratic forms, reflecting the prevailing conception of deities as the cause of all things. During the second, an age of imagination, nobility and pride dominated human nature, and the government was led by a warrior aristocracy. During this time, language, law, and culture developed, and mythic or poetic modes of consciousness became dominant. Finally, during the third, an age of reason, reflective rationality guided human behavior, and government took the form of egalitarian democracy. But Vico would not bask in pure optimism. He anticipated the possibility of a return to barbarism by imagining history as a spiral movement with cycles as part of the process.

For Vico, the proper means of studying history emanated from philosophy, that is, a system of reasoning from axioms, definitions, and postulates, and from philology, for him, the empirical study of the languages, history, and literature. Oddly, considering Vico's animus against Descartes, *The New Science* assumed the format of a geometry text, setting forth specific rules by which to obtain the truth. Among other things, he warned of prejudices conducive to error. Scholars should beware of exaggerating the grandeur of the past. They should understand that all nations favor their own history at the expense of others. They should not assume that people in the past resembled them or that the ancients knew more about themselves than current scholars. Vico proposed to employ the study of linguistics, mythology, and law as keys to unlock the meaning of the past. Historians could never comprehend their predecessors unless they learned to see the people as the people viewed themselves.

For this reason, Vico scrutinized the roots of words, folklore, tales, myths, legends, and legal systems for important clues. For Voltaire, a story about supernatural beings acting upon the human residents of the world signified ignorance and superstition. For Vico, it provided a means of investigating the conception those people held of themselves and their position in the universe. By emphasizing context and self-perception, Vico produced an early version of "historicism," which would take hold in the nineteenth century. While Enlightenment thinkers liberated history from the constrictions of theology, Vico and his followers discovered methods by which to recover the past. In the nineteenth century, their disciples obtained a modern consciousness.

History in the nineteenth century became multifaceted, diffuse, and rigorous methodologically. As a consequence, the study of history gained respectability in the great European universities of the day and achieved the status of an academic discipline. Professionally trained historians ultimately dominated the field, but gifted amateurs and philosophers with an interest in history also contributed to three kinds of historical writing. One grew out of the struggles of the French Revolution and the Napoleonic Wars and emphasized a romantic and nationalistic approach. A second, especially in Germany, treated history as a subject for abstract, philosophical thinking. A third, a forerunner of today's university-based, professional history, aspired to find out what actually happened through careful investigations in archives. The ensuing process enriched the discipline and overcame some of the incapacitating shortcomings of Enlightenment historiography. Rather than manifest disdain for the past, the historians of the nineteenth century reveled in its diversity.

Romantic and nationalistic historiography predominated in France after the Bourbon restoration in 1815. Jules Michelet, a disciple of Vico, aspired to write the history of the French people. While using sources such as folklore, songs, poetry, and architecture, he developed portraits of everyday life among the common people. His six-volume *History of France* eulogized peasant life and exulted in the emergence of nationalism. Related themes appeared in Francois Guizot's *History of Civilization in France*, published in 1830. This patriotic expression won fame for Guizot as a historian and also influence and power. He became the king's first minister under Louis Philippe. History and politics blended together nicely in Guizot's case.

In England, Thomas Babington Macaulay also favored romance. As a prose stylist he had few equals. High-blown and self-consciously magisterial in the approved fashion of the nineteenth century, Macaulay's *History of England* obtained a wide audience and established history as a branch of great literature. It also articulated an uncompromising version of the Whig interpretation of England's past by treating the nation's story as synonymous with the emergence of liberty. As Macaulay wrote, "The history of England is emphatically the history of progress. It is the history of a constant movement of a great society." In sonorous and balanced cadences, the historian argued the case, applauding the triumph of the Glorious Revolution of 1688 over the Stuart despots, concluding that "the history of our country . . . is eminently the history of physical, of moral, and of intellectual improvement."[7]

In the United States, the works of George Bancroft and Francis Parkman also set forth the themes of romantic nationalism. These great amateurs employed soaring prose for dramatic effects. Bancroft, like Guizot, combined careers in scholarship and public service. His story of national development emphasized the advance of liberty from the viewpoint of a Jeffersonian Democrat. In a series of books, Parkman's elegant prose reconstructed the conflict between France and Great Britain in North America during colonial times. Parkman's *The Oregon Trail*, another sort of adventure, was a kind of nature poem. In contrast, Henry Adams's nine-volume *History of the United States during the Jefferson and Madison Administrations* aspired to the status of science. As the grandson of one president, John Quincy Adams, and the great-grandson of another, John Adams, the cosmopolitan and well-connected Henry Adams wanted to tell the nation's story and also uncover the laws governing invariable relationships in human affairs. Although he later judged the second part of his effort a failure, his work still ranks as a foremost scholarly attainment.

Abstract forms of philosophical history emanated from Germany beginning in the eighteenth century. Johann Gottfried Herder and Immanuel Kant both wrote philosophical treatises on history. Herder's *Ideas toward a Philosophy of History of Man* described human life as closely related to nature and portrayed history as an evolutionary process. Each stage in the course of human development depended upon everything that had gone before. Otherwise, the latter stages could not occur at all. What existed in the present and what would come about in the future necessarily presumed whatever had been. This claim demolished the Enlightenment's habit of disparaging the past and compelled historians to appreciate the integrity of all eras. Herder celebrated the varieties of human experience and extrapolated an important observation from them. According to Collingwood, he was "the first thinker to recognize in a systematic way that there are differences between different kinds of men, and that human nature is not uniform but diversified."[8] This view anticipated Collingwood's own conviction that people have no fixed nature. Instead, they have their history and become whatever historical experience makes of them. Collingwood held that true historical thinking can never exist without this fundamental recognition.

Immanuel Kant reacted negatively to Herder's claims and wrote a critical response entitled "An Idea for a Universal History from a Cosmopolitan Point of View." As Herder's former teacher, Kant thought his student's work wrongheaded and in need of correction. Though never concerned primarily with the study of history, Kant too favored a philosophical treatment of the subject. Harkening back to Enlightenment traditions, he rejected Herder's emphasis on human dissimilarities and proposed instead to regard the unfolding of history as "the realization of a hidden plan of nature" by which "all the capacities implanted by her in mankind can be fully developed." Less impressed with diversity than Herder, Kant dwelled upon uniformity. For him, history amounted to a process by which humankind became rational and hence fulfilled its fundamental nature. With this view in mind, the main task of the philosophical historians was to comprehend the means and mechanisms for attaining this aim.

Georg Wilhelm Friedrich Hegel addressed the issue in an ornate body of writing intended to explain the whole of the experienced world. Defining nature and history as the manifestations of divine will in space and time, Hegel developed a complicated and inclusive philosophical system to make everything intelligible. Its very complexity defied summary and often put off practicing historians who doubted the usefulness and verifiability of Hegel's magnificent abstractions. His *Philosophy of History*, a series of lectures compiled and published after his death, pursued no less an ambition than to make the entirety of the human past comprehensible.

Hegel espoused profound religious commitments. In repudiation of Enlightenment thinking, he put God back into history through his interpretation of it as a logical and orderly process, the manifestation of divine will in time. As a consequence, the attributes of reason and freedom, identified as characteristics of divine spirit, would encompass the world. To make the point differently, Hegel wanted to provide a theodicy in which he would explain the ways of God in the world He had created. For Hegel, experienced reality existed first as an abstract ideal and later was made actual in the world through the unfolding of divine will in time.

In Hegel's scheme, the mechanism of change bringing about the realization of divine will proceeded dialectically, and human minds could arrive at understanding by reasoning similarly. In his world of pure thought, all things gave rise to their opposites. Light had no meaning apart from dark. The same held true for high and low, sharp and dull, near and far. In like fashion, an idea, or a thesis, resulted in a counterproposition, or antithesis, and the ensuing debate produced a synthesis, which in turn became a thesis and set the whole process in motion again. For Hegel, the dialectic not only characterized how thought progressed toward understanding but also how change actually took place in the material world. Confusingly, he added that the steps could take place out of logical sequence.

The march of history, nevertheless, produced changing levels of consciousness among human beings. In effect, their natures underwent alterations as a result of new forms of experience and awareness. To put it simplistically, they became more rational and freer. As Hegel explained, people could not attain the ends of history, that is, freedom and rationality, until they knew that they possessed the capacity to exercise such faculties. This consciousness dawned slowly. As Hegel observed, "The East knew and to the present days knows only that *One* is free [i.e., the oriental despot]; the Greek and Roman world, that *Some* are free [i.e., the aristocratic elite]; the German World knows that *All* are free [under the legal structure of the monarchy]."[9]

Though Hegel believed that he had explained the forms and logic of historical development with proper regard for the facts, not many practicing historians ever adopted the Hegelian system or tried to work within its constraints. Nevertheless, Hegel significantly influenced historical thinking in the nineteenth century. Most obviously, though Hegel shared with Kant an inclination to emphasize emergent rationality among humans, in many ways an equivalent of freedom, he also sided with Herder in his comprehension of human nature as malleable and never fixed or final. It existed in a condition of becoming. Accordingly, different humans in different times and places had different natures. Hegel also favored Herder's holistic conception of the human past in which each phase possessed integrity as a prerequisite to whatever followed. For Hegel, the patronizing attitudes of the Enlightenment could only distort the past and prevent true understanding. He insisted that historians must study bygone ages and epochs on their own terms.

These two points became central assertions in a school of historical thinking in nineteenth-century Germany called "historicism." An awkward translation of the German word *historismus*, this approach affirmed the need for particular methodological means to fathom the meaning of the past. Fundamentally, it pointed to the diversity of human experience and claimed that different people viewed the world differently. To comprehend the past, scholars had to enter into the mental universe of past actors empathetically and reconstruct their picture of reality. Only by putting the past in context could scholars credibly explain various forms of behavior. Knowledge of how the historical actors thought would facilitate an understanding of how they acted.

German historicists operated out of universities and spent their time in archives working with documents. By and large, they accepted Hegel's methodological advice but ignored or rejected his larger metaphysical system. It probably struck them as an a priori invention, neither proven nor provable. Rather than embark upon a philosophically grandiose venture, most of them embraced the more modest aim of writing history as it actually happened. One of the foremost practitioners of this method, Leopold von Ranke, wanted to describe historical events "as they really were." More than anyone, he transformed history into a modern academic discipline, university-based, archive-bound, and professional in that the leading proponents underwent extensive postgraduate training. The methods and techniques emanating from Germany spread elsewhere on the continent, to Great Britain, and to the United States. They called for extensive research in primary sources to discover the truth, for detached and unbiased judgment, and for a determination by historians to see and to experience the world as it seemed to the historical actors.

Ranke's body of work staggers the imagination. He lived ninety years and produced sixty published volumes. As the inventor of modern history, he chose the emergence of the European state system after the Reformation as his subject. Working out of the University of Berlin for fifty years, his seminar method of instruction and his prolific scholarship made him world famous. George Bancroft of the United States on one occasion called him "the greatest living historian." Ranke stated his purpose in the preface to his *Histories of the Latin and Germanic Nations from 1494–1514.* "History has been assigned the office of judging the past, of instructing our times for the benefit of future years. This essay does not aspire to such high offices; it only wants to show how it had really been—*wie es eigentlich gewesen.*"[10]

Ranke aspired to achieve balance and objectivity. Though on occasion his personal commitments to monarchy, Protestantism, and the Prussian nation state may have colored his judgments, his biases seldom destroyed his impartiality. Indeed, his works retain believability in the present day because of his comprehensive research and scholarly disengagement. His masterpiece, *History of the Popes*, aroused criticism among contemporaries who thought it too bland and balanced. He also displayed great breadth. At age eighty-three, he set out to compose a universal history and managed to get through the fifteenth century before his death in 1885. Ranke's great legacy persisted into the twentieth century and has profoundly shaped the professional writing of history.

Another strain of German thinking also retains an impact in the present day. As a young man, Karl Marx came under the influence of Hegel's idealism while pursuing advanced studies in philosophy at the University of Berlin. Though enamored of the dialectical construct as a logical device for describing change, Marx rejected the abstract and ethereal character of the Hegelian system. For Marx, reality resided in the physical world and not in idealistic forms as Hegel believed. According to Marx, Hegel's philosophy was backward. Throughout his life, Marx aimed at rebutting Hegel's idealism with a new system of philosophical understanding based on dialectical materialism. For him, this system provided a way of comprehending the processes of historical change and established a basis for predicting the future.

Marx focused his attention on work, that is, the activity by which people obtained their livelihoods. He also examined the ensuing relationships with the means of production. Two ideas figured prominently in his thinking. For Marx, the reality of the class struggle characterized the whole of human experience. In addition, a labor theory of value provided an essential key. Marx distinguished between the privileged elites who controlled the agencies of production and the unprivileged masses who labored in the fields and factories. According to him, exploitation inevitably followed, because the former always appropriated a disproportionately large share of the wealth created by the invest-ment of the workers' labor. For Marx, goods and commodities took on value because of the work required to make them. Farmers and workers produced valuable things and then had the proceeds taken away from them because of inequitable class relationships.

Much of Marx's writing sought to demonstrate the validity of his claims through investigations into the operation of European capitalism. His works also set forth predictions. The unfolding of history would bring about deliverance from want and oppression through the creation of a society without classes and exploitation. According to his explication, human experience consisted of a sequence of tumultuous upheavals in which evolv-ing technologies overturned established systems of production by rendering them obsolete and undoing existing economic, social, and political relationships. Change, the enduring constant, proceeded dialectically, bringing human beings ever closer to a more perfect future, described by Marx as a condition in which all people would share more evenly in the rewards of their work. His vision of the future drew upon traditions in philosophy of history going back to the Jews and the early Christians, but in his rendition, the course of secular history rather than transcendence would bring about salvation. Affirming a linear and progressive view of historical development, Marx made philosophy of history serve the cause of revolution. As he once remarked, "The philoso-phers have only *interpreted* the world, in various ways; the point, however, is to *change* it."[11]

The Marxist injunction created immense divisions in the modern world over the proper understanding of politics, economics, and the role of history. While Marx and his followers issued the call to revolu-tionary action and sought legitimation in historical imperatives, more conventional and traditional scholars held back from such leaps, refus-ing to employ their mode of investigation to justify a particular vision of the future. Trained by graduate schools in the importance of archival research and methodological and conceptual rigor, they hesitated to extrapolate predictions about the future from their findings, preferring to restrict their professional interests to presumably knowable subjects. Most historians left the predictive function to philosophers of history, while others as believers in the analytical powers of Marxism used them to examine the workings of capitalism and the class struggle.

Two British historians E.P. Thompson in *The Making of the English Working Class* (1963) and Eric Hobsbawm in his many books earned special acclaim.

RECOMMENDED READINGS

Historians at Work, Vol. 2: *From Valla to Gibbon*, and Vol. 3: *Niebuhr to Maitland*, eds. Peter Gay and Victor G. Wexler (New York: Harper and Row, 1972, 1975), make available samples of the writings of the great historians. Herbert Butterfield, *The Origins of History* (New York: Basic Books, 1981), traces the process of secularization. Additional commentary appears in Paul K. Conkin and Roland N. Stromberg, *The Heritage and Challenge of History* (New York: Dodd, Mead and Co., 1971). R. G. Collingwood's, *The Idea of History* (New York: Oxford University Press, 1956) is indispensable. A revised edition of this work, edited and introduced by Jan Van Der Dussen (Oxford: Clarendon Press, 1993), includes previously unpublished lectures from the period 1926 to 1928. *History and Historians in the Nineteenth Century* by G.P. Gooch (Boston: Beacon Press, 1959, first published in 1913) and *The Theory and Practice of History* by Leopold von Ranke, eds. Georg C. Iggers and Konrad von Moltke (New York: Bobbs-Merrill Company, 1973), vividly depict developments during "the golden age" and make them accessible to English-language readers. Leonard Krieger's, *Ranke: The Meaning of History* (Chicago: University of Chicago Press, 1977) is a sophisticated intellectual biography using psychohistorical techniques. Interested readers will also benefit from *Leopold von Ranke and the Shaping of the Historical Discipline* (Syracuse University Press, 1990), eds. Georg C. Iggers and James M. Powell. John Clive's *Not By Fact Alone: Essays on the Writing and Reading of History* (Boston: Houghton Mifflin, 1989) is a delightful justification for reading the great historians of the nineteenth century. B. A. Haddock, *An Introduction to Historical Thought* (London: Edward Arnold Publishers, 1980), surveys modern historical thinking and addresses the question of whether the models of natural science provide an apt basis for studying history. In contrast, Hayden White, *Metahistory: The Historical Imagination in Nineteenth-Century Europe* (Baltimore: Johns Hopkins University Press, 1973), argues the case that literary conventions shape historical narratives. Joyce Appleby, Lynn Hunt, and Margaret Jacob's, *Telling the Truth about History* (New York: W. W. Norton, 1994) contains an illuminating discussion of science and history as ways of knowing.

Useful works on specific historians include Ross King's, *Machiavelli, Philosopher of Power* (New York: HarperCollins, 2007); Roy Porter's, *Gibbon: Making History* (New York: St. Martin's Press, 1988); Patricia B. Cradock's, *Edward Gibbon: Luminous Historian, 1772–1794* (Baltimore: Johns Hopkins

University Press, 1989); Nicolas Phillipson's, *Hume* (New York: St. Martin's Press, 1989); Arthur Mitzman's, *Michelet, Historian: Rebirth and Romanticism in Nineteenth-Century France* (New Haven: Yale University Press, 1990); John Clive's, *Macaulay: The Shaping of the Historian* (New York: Alfred A. Knopf, 1973); and Owen Dudley Edwards' *Macaulay* (New York: St. Martin's Press, 1988). Herbert Butterfield's, *The Whig Interpretation of History* (London: Penguin Books, 1931), remains illuminating. Isaiah Berlin's, *Vico and Herder: Two Studies in the History of Ideas* (New York: Viking Press, 1976); and Mark Lilla's, *G. B. Vico: The Making of an Anti-Modern* (Cambridge, MA: Harvard University Press, 1993) establish appropriate intellectual contexts. Part III, "Early Modern Historiography," in the *Companion to Historiography* (New York: Routledge, 1997) is most illuminating. Similarly, John Burrow's, *A History of Histories: Epics, Chronicles, Romances and Inquiries from Herodotus and Thucydides to the Twenties Century* (New York: Alfred E. Knopf, 2008) is indispensable.

ENDNOTES

1. B. A. Haddock, *An Introduction to Historical Thought* (London: Edward Arnold, 1980), 45.
2. R. G. Collingwood, *The Idea of History* (New York: Oxford University Press, 1956), 76.
3. Peter Gay and Victor G. Wexler, eds., *Historians at Work*, Vol. 2: *Valla to Gibbon* (New York: Harper and Row, 1972), 84.
4. Collingwood, *Idea of History*, 77.
5. From "The Age of Louis XIV," in Gay and Wexler, eds., *Historians at Work*, 2:285.
6. Quoted in Gay and Wexler, eds., *Historians at Work*, 2:357. From Edward Gibbon, *The Decline and Fall of the Roman Empire*, abr. Moses Hadas (New York: Capricorn Books, 1962), 131.
7. Quoted in Gay and Wexler, eds., *Historians at Work*, Vol. 3: *Niebuhr to Maitland* (New York: Harper and Row, 1975), 89; Thomas Babington Macaulay, *The History of England: From the Accession of James II*, 5 vols. (New York: A. L. Burt Co., n.d.), 1:2–3.
8. Collingwood, *Idea of History*, 90–91.
9. From the introduction to Hegel's, *Philosophy of History*, in Monroe G. Beardsley, ed., *The European Philosophers from Descartes to Nietzsche* (New York: Modern Library, 1960), 553.
10. Quoted in Gay and Wexler, eds., *Historians at Work*, 3:16; Leopold von Ranke, *The Theory and Practice of History*, eds. Georg G. Iggers and Konrad von Moltke (New York: Bobbs-Merrill, 1973), 137.
11. Quoted in Bruce Mazlish, *The Riddle of History: The Great Speculators from Vico to Freud* (New York: Minerva Press, 1966), 227.

4

PHILOSOPHY OF HISTORY: SPECULATIVE APPROACHES

The term *philosophy of history* has acquired several connotations during the past three centuries. When Voltaire coined the term by insisting upon doing history *en philosophe,* he meant the construction of more meaningful narratives through the exercise of thoughtful reflection. Later the term took on different definitions. One version of the philosophy of history referred to speculation over the course of history. This approach, the subject of this chapter, sought to obtain profound levels of truth by discerning patterns in the past and connecting them with expectations for the future. It required explanations that would aid in foretelling the goals and purposes of history on the supposition that students of history could know such things. A second version, the analytical philosophy of history addressed in the next chapter, focused on problems in methodology, particularly in the areas of logic and epistemology. This approach has set forth rigorous standards and sometimes has scrutinized the degree to which historians and their actual practices have measured up. Both renditions, while emphasizing imaginative inquiry guided always by fairness, reason, and evidence, have contributed to the intellectual richness of the discipline.

Human beings have ruminated about the directions of history since ancient times. Among other things, they have sought to mute their sense of vulnerability in facing the unknown by seeking to determine recurring tendencies in the past. Over the years, at least three basic schemata have characterized such endeavors: the cyclical, the providential, and the progressive. To be sure, variations on each have occurred, and the three views sometimes overlap and intermingle. In spite of such confusion, each view retained a measure of distinctiveness. In the first, history moves in circles, repeating endlessly over and over again. In the second and the third views, history follows a linear process moving through time from a beginning to a middle to an end. The providential and the progressive versions each presumed some kind of advancement, or progress, through time but portrayed the impetus for change differently. In the providential view, divine guidance moved history along. In the progressive view, natural or metaphysical forces provided the momentum.

The cyclical idea arose among ancient peoples and in some Eastern cultures. Egyptians, Sumerians, Babylonians, and Greeks derived the premise from the orderly and predictable fluctuations of nature and attached scant significance to the passage of events. In a sense, they refused history. As noted by the historian of religions Mircea Eliade in his book *Cosmos and History: The Myth of the Eternal Return*, the inhabitants of traditional or "archaic" societies lived and operated in a kind of timeless present, a world very different from that apprehended by Jews and Christians. Though cyclical interpretations persisted even into the twentieth century, for example, in a dazzling and perplexing work entitled *The Decline of the West* by Oswald Spengler, a German philosopher and historian, the more characteristic form of thinking in Western civilization has emphasized linear conceptions of the past.

A belief in providential design, affirmed so exhaustively by St. Augustine in the fifth century, appeared incessantly in the historical writing of the Middle Ages. This approach brought coherence to medieval chronicles by providing the means to fit contemporary records into the flow of universal history and also to express the faith in the reality of God's presence and purpose in the world. Sometimes unique formulations resulted in dramatic twists. Late in the twelfth century, Joachim de Flora divided history into three epochs, each corresponding with a figure in the Holy Trinity. The Age of the Father encompassed the pre-Christian era, the Age of the Son, the Christian era, and the Age of the Holy Spirit, an anticipation of things to come. According to Joachim, each period would endure for forty generations, and the passage from one to the next would signify advancement toward a condition of greater wisdom, love, spirituality, and happiness. The prophecy ironically took on revolutionary political implications after Joachim's death in 1202 by sparking interest among poor and humble people who aspired to a better life and promoted an upsurge of religious millenarianism, that is, the expectation of 1,000 years of joy, serenity, prosperity, and justice.

A tripartite division of the past also appeared in Giambattista Vico's *The New Science*. A devout Roman Catholic, Vico tried to combine his belief in Divine Providence with a scholarly insistence upon the need for empirical investigations. By demonstrating the facts in particular cases, he would confirm the veracity of the larger whole. In his scheme of things, an amalgam of many elements, history advanced progressively through stages but also fluctuated in cycles, resulting in a kind of spiral effect. Vico perceived a three-tiered progression from "the age of the gods" to "the age of heroes" to "the age of men," and in each he detected holistic relationships among institutions, practices, and beliefs. In the first stage, "the gentiles believed they lived under divine governments and everything was commanded them by auspices and oracles." In the second, "heroes . . . reigned everywhere in aristocratic commonwealths, on account of a superiority of nature which they held themselves to have," and in the third, "all men recognized themselves as equal in human nature and therefore there were established first the popular commonwealths and then the monarchies, both of which are forms of human government."[1]

Vico's extrapolation from these representations held that special forms of government—theocratic, aristocratic, republican, or monarchical—corresponded to each change, and that particular kinds of language and jurisprudence necessarily resulted. For Vico, the various cultural parts interlocked at each stage, forming a coherent and uniform whole. In a summary statement, he further claimed that transformations took place in the makeup of human beings. In his view, "the nature of peoples is first crude, then severe, then benign, then delicate, finally dissolute." The cycles necessarily would run the whole course, each giving cultural expression to successive changes and then recurring on a higher plane, resulting in a progressive movement under God's supervision.

In the nineteenth century, Georg Wilhelm Friedrich Hegel endorsed some similar propositions. Indeed, he calculated the parts of his philosophical system to demonstrate the creative immanence of divine power in space and time. Nature and history for him served up the testimony. In what may have amounted to the most ambitious philosophical treatment of history ever attempted, Hegel set forth a dynamic and rational process aimed at the attainment of reason and freedom. For Hegel, the course of history moved by comprehensible means toward this goal in a dialectical fashion. The mechanisms of historical change required that ideas, or mind, generate reality by giving rise to opposites so that a constant tug-of-war went on between that which actually existed and that which might come about.

According to Hegel, history consisted of the means by which God achieved his purposes in the world and human beings arrived at new and higher levels of consciousness, both of their surroundings and of their own capabilities. The course of development moved generally from East to West from the Orient through the intervening regions to Western Europe and took on institutional forms in the great religions and the apparatus of the state. Hegel espoused a provincial Eurocentric view, excluding Africa, the New World, and the Slavic domains from the course of history on the grounds that the inhabitants had made scant contributions to the progress of humankind. In contrast, Greece, Rome, and Germany had participated conspicuously. Hegel assigned special importance to "World Heroes," his term for great men, who through the pursuit of their own interests actually served larger purposes ordained by the Deity. In quest of personal empire, Napoleon promoted European progress by sweeping away feudal remnants. Hegel attributed the unintended outcome to "the cunning of reason," his phrase for the capacity of divine power to manipulate historical actors in service to its own purposes.

The power of Hegel's intellect resulted in formidable attainments. His system described a theodicy, that is, a justification of God's way toward humankind. Also, in Hegel's view, the system conformed to empirical proofs. But more practical-minded historians regarded such constructs as the result not of hard facts but of unproven assumptions and a priori reasoning. The overwhelming inclusiveness of Hegel's philosophy of history, that is, his fierce determination to account for all things, would have placed unbearable strains on more orthodox historians seeking to work within such constraints. Very few scholars ever tried to compose their narratives within the confines of Hegel's mental universe. Nevertheless, his contribution to historical thinking figured prominently, particularly in the emergent German historicist school, by depicting the flow of history as successive changes in the level of consciousness among human beings.

A shift toward secular characterizations of the past in progressive, linear terms achieved particular prominence during the Age of Enlightenment in the eighteenth century. Typically, these approaches set forth a preferred and favored vision of the future by which to bring about human redemption and then showed the necessary mechanisms driving history in that direction. The French contributed two notable exemplars. Voltaire explained history as a movement away from ignorance and superstition toward rationality and enlightenment. Somewhat similarly, in a work entitled *Sketch for a Historical Picture of the Progress of the Human Mind,* Marie Jean Antoine Condorcet early in the 1790s anticipated idyllic conditions at the end of ten developing historic stages, eventuating in "the abolition of inequality between nations, the progress of equality within each nation, and the true perfections of mankind."[2]

German thinkers also harbored progressive expectations. Immanuel Kant's "Idea for a Universal History from a Cosmopolitan Point of View" produced an important statement. Published in 1784, a decade before Condorcet's *Sketch,* this essay affirmed the expansion of freedom as the overriding purpose of history. According to Kant's argument, "the history of mankind viewed as a whole, can be regarded as the realization of a hidden plan of nature" to bring about the requisite political conditions both within states and among them so that "all the capacities implanted by her nature in mankind can be fully developed."[3] Although vague in explaining the specifics, Kant envisioned the creation of an international league of nations as the prime institutional means by which to achieve order and rationality within the world under law.

For Kant, the study of history was not a central preoccupation. Nevertheless, according to the nine propositions set forth in this short piece, history moved inexorably toward the goal of liberty as a consequence of what Kant called "unsocial sociability." This energizing principle, really the driving force of progress, resembled Hegel's idea, "the cunning of reason." Such formulations expressed a favorite notion of Enlightenment philosophers, who liked to think that the pursuit of private interests would somehow automatically translate into the advancement of the collective good. Kant intended the term "unsocial sociability" to typify the devices employed by nature "to bring about the development of all the capacities implanted in men." He used the term to characterize a complicated process serving the general welfare in which social dynamics balanced countervailing tendencies toward integration and disintegration. As he explained in the fourth proposition, the tendency of human beings "to enter into society" appeared in conjunction with "an accompanying resistance which continually threatens to dissolve this society."[4] The ensuing creative tension resulted in progress.

To put this claim another way, the conflicting and contradictory human needs to live together and to assert individual integrity paradoxically provided the momentum to move ahead. Typical of his time, Kant regarded stories about the past as lamentable tales of chaos, woe, disorder, and suffering. Nevertheless, he hoped for a better future and intended his essay to hasten it along. In all likelihood, he wanted his writing to function as a kind of self-fulfilling prophecy, as suggested by his choice of language in the eighth proposition. There he made no claim that history is the realization of a hidden plan of nature but rather said that it "can be regarded" as such. By implanting this thought, possibly he hoped to encourage rational beings to act upon it as though it were true and thereby to attain the larger aim.

Another prophetic version appeared in the works of Karl Marx and his collaborator, Friedrich Engels. Also linear and progressive in conception, their writings had an enduring and provocative effect. Unlike Kant, who only dabbled in the study of history, Marx and Engels devoted a large portion of their lives to the endeavor and from it fashioned a theory of change and revolution. Characteristically, they too devised a vision of a more perfect future, but unlike utopians, visionaries, and metaphysicians, whom they scorned as fantasists, Marx and Engels believed that their analyses and predictions originated not in a priori imaginings but in true comprehension of reality and scientific understanding of historical development.

Their approach centered on the material world as the proper object of study, particularly the technologies of production and the economic, political, and social relationships generated by them. For Marx and Engels, the ownership of the means of production, that is, tools, land, and factories, formed the main determinant of everything else. Second, Marx and Engels focused on class, defined in economic terms as ownership of property or the lack thereof. As affirmed in *The Communist Manifesto*, their thesis held that all history has been "the history of class struggles" between the dominant and the dominated classes at various stages of development.[5]

Similarly Eurocentric, the Marx and Engels formulation resembled Hegel's by depicting the movement of history from the East (Asia) to the West (Europe) and resulting in the expansion of human consciousness. Marx reversed Hegel's view by vesting reality in the material rather than the ideal world, but he accepted the dialectic as the means of change. Thus the term "dialectical materialism" is used to describe Marx's system. His subsequent division of the past into four great epochs had less to do with actual time periods than with his understanding of the various sets of human relationships in different systems of economic production.

The overarching pattern discerned by Marx concerned the exploitation of working people. Throughout history, it set the haves, the wealthy and powerful, against the have-nots, the poor and vulnerable. Systematic and institutional methods amounting to thievery allowed the former to relieve the latter of the just rewards of their labor. For Marx, the amount of work invested in anything established its true value, but under the prevailing conditions the members of the labor force never received their just recompense. Instead, the ruling class appropriated the riches for its own use.

Marx posited the existence in the beginning of time of an age of primitive communism, marked by Garden-of-Eden–like qualities such as simplicity, equality, and communal sharing, but then the advent of private property, the Marxian equivalent of original sin, shattered the idyll. Subsequently in Asia during the age of oriental despotism, populations concentrated in small, dispersed communities under absolute rulers. Marx regarded such forms as lifeless artifacts, receptive only to change imposed from the outside. His main ideas centered on Greece, Rome, and Western Europe, from which he derived a model of progress moving from the ancient to the medieval to the modern world. In ancient times, the class struggle took place in city-states and set slave owners against slaves. In the Middle Ages, feudalism engaged lords against serfs. In Marx's own day, the interests of the bourgeoisie, the owners of production, conflicted with the aspirations of wage laborers, the proletarians, and ultimately would lead to communist revolutions, the abolition of private property, and a new age of freedom and equality in which the formerly exploited classes would share justly in the rewards for their labors. Marx's depictions of the past and his expectations for the future provoked storms of criticism. Critics claimed that his understanding of the ancient and medieval worlds contained fundamental flaws and that his views overrated the potential for revolution in modern times. Yet, for radical thinkers his vision still has the power to captivate. Marx knew more about nineteenth-century capitalism than almost anyone, and his depiction of technology as an impetus for economic change conveys an essential insight.

According to his argument, the ruling class in each stage of historical development, that is, the males in charge of production, also obtained control of political, legal, and social structures in order to safeguard their positions. For him, government officials made up the board of directors of the economic rulers. Similarly, legal arrangements, the social structure, and most other forms of organized human intercourse reflected the unequal distribution of economic power. At the same time, the dynamism of historical imperatives threatened to unwork the status quo. Time and again, new technologies destabilized existing relationships and produced upheavals, rendering the old structures obsolete. When the owners of factories obtained economic power, the former ruling elites, the feudal lords, struggled to retain their control of the political, legal, and social systems but could not. The very logic of history had doomed them. Once triumphant, the bourgeoisie erected institutional defense in support of their ascendancy.

For Marx, all historical eras gave rise to class exploitation, but had legitimacy as a necessary step in the march toward communism. The attainment of perfection could never ensue without the necessary prerequisites. For Marx, the model achieved truth from empirical proof and also from the irrefutable force of its logic. For skeptics, Marx's prophetic faith held less interest than his holistic analysis of political economy and the processes of historical change. Some critics went so far as to agree that they need not embrace all of Marx in order to profit from his explication of the workings of economic capitalism.

Old-fashioned, speculative philosophy of history lost some of its appeal in the twentieth century, in part because of its traditional grandiose aims. In an age of specialized inquiry in which, according to a well-known quip, we learn more and more about less and less, hard-nosed observers put little faith in attempts to account for the whole of the human past. Indeed, they regarded such endeavors as silly or contemptible enterprises based on pure imagination and incapable of proof or demonstration. Although many scholars turned their attention to other things, the older versions of speculative history lived on, oftentimes in modified forms. Marxian legacies amalgamated with the ideas of Vladimir I. Lenin and retained an intellectual and revolutionary appeal in various quarters around the world. Oswald Spengler and Arnold Toynbee composed universal and philosophical histories. Sigmund Freud produced a body of speculative writing with significance for historians, and religious thinkers such as Reinhold Niebuhr took an approach to history that evoked memories of St. Augustine.

In the twentieth century, Marxist ideology became the official version of the past in communist countries and purported to present hopes for a better future in others. In hybrid form with Leninism, it held importance as a theory of international relations according to which modern capitalist nation-states act in the world arena primarily for economic reasons. Seeking cheap resources, investment outlets for surplus capital, and new markets to relieve overproduction at home, the capitalist powers according to this critique would always engage in a chronic struggle for profit and advantage, sometimes colliding in armed conflict, until the victory of revolution would sweep away all need for such practices. During the 1960s a group of historians in the United States called "the New Left" challenged orthodox accounts of American foreign relations by arguing that Marxist–Leninist models facilitated insight into the international behavior of the United States. According to this view, the idea of U.S. exceptionalism, that is, a conception of moral superiority over Euro-pean standards, lacked validity. In Cold War studies, a vociferous debate over the origins occasioned polemical duels when radicals claimed that expansive U.S. capitalism contributed significantly to the collapse of the wartime alliance with the Soviet Union. Similarly, a debate over "dependency theory" as an explanation for the plight of poor countries in the developing world became intense. Initially a product of Marxist–Leninist thinking in Latin America, dependency theory attributed the pervasiveness of poverty and underdevelop-ment to the requirements of a global capitalist system designed to drain away wealth from the provincial and colonial regions to the advanced metropolis. According to this analysis, the world capitalist system will always cause oppression and exploitation. Although the termination of the Cold War has now altered the context of this discussion, questions of development and modernization retain crucial significance in connection with famine, genocide, trade, global warning, and shortages of fossil fuel.

Similarly, Oswald Spengler, a morose, brilliant, eccentric, and pessimistic German prophet from the era of the First World War, entertained no visions of progress and salvation. The title in English of his erudite two-volume work sets the tone. *The Decline of the West* resurrected the cyclical view of history while arguing that no means existed for escaping the dictates of destiny. Spengler identified culture as the proper unit of historical study. Though vague in defining the meaning, he depicted eight cultures over the course of human history. He called them the Indian, Babylonian, Chinese, Egyptian, Mexican, Arabic, Classical, and Western. For him, the distinguishing feature of a culture formed "a single, singularly constituted soul." In an imaginative mystical flight, he proclaimed, "A Culture is born in the moment when a great soul awakens out of the protospirituality of ever-childish humanity, and detaches itself, a form from the formless, a bounded and mortal thing from the boundless and enduring." He elaborated, "It blooms on the soil of an exactly-definable landscape, to which plant-wise it remains bound. It dies when this soul has actualized the full sum of its possibilities in the shape of peoples, languages, dogmas, arts, states, sciences, and reverts into proto-soul."[6]

Spengler regarded culture as the analogue of an organism in the biological world, fated to pass through the phases of birth, youth, maturity, old age, and death. Sometimes, as an alternative, he used the phases of spring, summer, fall, and winter to describe the growth of culture. Each culture had a life span of about 1,000 years. Spengler proposed to study cultures through the use of comparative morphology. This term, derived from the study of anatomy, referred to the form and structure of living organisms. Through the use of such techniques, Spengler intended to move beyond shallow comparisons to profounder insights. By this method, he concluded, Napoleon and Alexander the Great represented morphological "contemporaries" in that both stood in the same phase of a declining culture.

Spengler distinguished among the various cultures on the basis of diverse conceptions of time and space. An expression of cultural determinism, Spengler's provocative approach stated that each culture dictated a different standard for perceiving and measuring time and space. Each culture thereby obtained uniqueness, but at the same time the human beings in any one of them experienced isolation from all the others. Spengler put little stock in the possibility of meaningful cross-cultural transfers. Such efforts could only produce inexplicabil-ity. To work out the ramifications, he concentrated on three cultures, the Classical, the Arabic, and the Western, whose "souls" he character-ized as Apollinian, Magian, and Faustian.

Spengler described the prevailing conceptions of time and space within each culture and then employed illustrations from the worlds of mathematics, drama, architecture, politics, economics, and so forth to substantiate his claims. According to him, the Classical, or Apollinian, soul cherished most the qualities of closed space and timelessness in the present and attained those ideals preeminently in nude statuary and Euclidean geometry. The Arabic, or Magian, soul organized impressions around a sense of cavernous space and time spans with a clear beginning and end. As examples, Spengler cited the early Christian caves, Muslim mosques, and the Judeo-Christian linear designs of history. Finally, the Western, or Faustian, soul conceived of pure and limitless space and time stretching out into infinity, represented by differential calculus, museums, clocks, and presumably space shots to Mars.

Whatever the observable variations, according to Spengler, all cultures share a common fate. Destiny requires that they run their life course and die. On this point, Spengler curiously used the language of astrology. In the German title of his work, *Der Untergang Des Abendlandes*, the first word has astrological significance, suggesting the decline or setting of the sun. As noted by one commentator, Bruce Mazlish, Spengler's sense of inevitability required foreordained outcomes because they are "in our stars." Mazlish referred to Spengler as "an astrological historian" for whom "real history is heavy with fate but free of laws." As Mazlish remarked, "We can *divine* the future but not reckon or calculate it."[7]

Such bizarre oddities abounded in Spengler's writing. Though Spengler possessed a doctoral degree, he never obtained an academic appointment and carried out his endeavors as an independent scholar. Perhaps his status as an outsider, removed from the mainstream of intellectual life in the universities, accounted for some of his quirks. His contemptuous disdain for other scholars and his pretentious boasts of an originality never previously attained rubbed readers the wrong way. But Spengler's pessimistic mood struck a chord with others in the years after the First World War and signaled a dramatic shift away from the sentimental optimism of the Victorian age.

Arnold Toynbee, an Englishman and a contemporary of Spengler, also experienced the historical trauma of the Great War. Seeking to render historical study more systematic, he inaugurated an ambitious project in 1920. Completed in 1954, Toynbee's twelve-volume work surveyed the whole experience of humankind and set forth a series of general propositions about its meaning. *A Study of History* paralleled Spengler's book in some respects but diverged in others. Notably, Toynbee developed an interest in exploring the origins of civilizations and claimed to arrive at conclusions by adhering to the requirements of English empiricism, that is, by allowing the evidence to direct his findings and speak for itself. Though Toynbee professed an aversion to the a priori techniques of his German counterpart, his critics later flailed him for falling far short of the aim, charging that he unwarrantably designated the Greek and Roman worlds as the models of all civilization and that he twisted the evidence to make it fit his preconceived theories.

Toynbee sought high levels of generality by presenting "societies" or "civilizations" as the proper units of historical study. Toynbee preferred them to nations or periods because they represented a more intelligible, larger whole. Though his vague definitions of these terms and discrepancies in usage can affect the count, Toynbee detected nineteen or twenty-one civilizations during the preceding 6,000 years. Five are still alive: our own Western civilization and also the Orthodox Christian, the Islamic, the Hindu, and the Far Eastern. The nonliving included the Hellenic, Syriac, Indic, Minoan, Sumeric, Hittite, Babylonic, Andean, Mexic, Yucatec, Mayan, and Egyptian. Finally, two sets of "fossilized" relics, the Jewish and Buddhist traditions, maintained remnants in the present. Toynbee reasoned that a majority of civilizations emerged from some kind of a predecessor and that others developed directly from primitive life. The problem of explaining the genesis especially intrigued him. He rejected racial considerations and circumstances of nature as inadequate in accounting for the change and proposed instead the concept of "challenge and response." As observed by D. C. Somervell, who abridged Toynbee's mighty work into two more accessible volumes:

> A survey of the great myths in which the wisdom of the human race is enshrined suggests the possibility that man achieves civilization not as a result of superior biological endowment or geographical environment, but as a response to a challenge in a situation of special difficulty which rouses him to make a hitherto unprecedented effort.[8]

In Toynbee's analysis, civilizations took shape when demanding challenges brought forth creative human responses. Toynbee emphasized the importance of "the golden mean." Too severe a challenge could overwhelm all manner of reactions and render them futile. Conversely, too bland a challenge would obviate any need to generate a response. According to Toynbee, the ease of life in the South Pacific failed to elicit a response leading to high levels of civilization. In contrast, the settlement efforts of Viking emigrants from Norway, which succeeded in Iceland, subsequently collapsed in Greenland upon encountering even tougher conditions.

Growth within a civilization, according to Toynbee, occurred when successive challenges met with creative responses. The responsibility for devising them resided with "creative minorities," that is, small groups of talented people who inspired others to follow them with the force of their example. The ensuing process, dubbed "mimesis" by Toynbee, impelled the masses of people to imitate their natural leaders. When mimesis ceased to exist or the minority elite lost its creativity, then "a time of troubles" descended upon society, suggesting the possibility of a breakdown.

Toynbee rejected strictly deterministic solutions to the problem. The disintegration of societies was not inevitable. Nevertheless, his scrutiny of the process showed that the transformation of a creative minority into merely a dominant minority and the emergence of an internal proletariat, which felt "in" but not "of" the society, signaled an impending schism. Though spiritual resources always have done a great deal to dictate the outcome, Toynbee thought that social decomposition came about not in a uniform fashion but by an alteration of "routs" and "rallies," his terms for defeats and recoveries. As Toynbee explained, the establishment of a universal state, such as the Roman Empire, represented a rally after a rout in a time of troubles, and the dissolution of a universal state indicated the final rout. Somewhat oddly, Toynbee believed that he had detected a rhythm in the process, consisting of three and a half beats: "rout-rally-rout-rally-rout-rally-rout." Claiming to have confirmed the pattern through his investigations into several extinct civilizations, he wondered whether it applied to his own. In the abridgment, Somervell suggested that it might by remarking, "As differentiation is the mark of growth, so standardization is the mark of disintegration."[9]

In Toynbee's last four volumes, religious themes became a dominant motif. Though convinced that his own civilization had advanced far into a time of troubles, thereby heralding the possibility of a decline and fall, he retained some hope that spiritual rebirth might halt the descent through the affirmation of a more creative alternative. In this philosophy of history, no deterministic laws compelled any particular outcome. Everything depended upon the human actors, and religious conviction would function as a prime arbiter. In his concluding volumes, Toynbee emerged more as a religious thinker than as a historian.

A quite different influence upon the philosophy of history took shape early in the twentieth century in the writings of Sigmund Freud. As the founder of psychoanalysis, Freud was not primarily a historian. Nevertheless, Freud developed an approach to the study of human behavior with implications for history. Rather than concentrate on large collectivities, such as "cultures" or "civilization," he worked as a therapist, counseling individual patients and then extending his findings and insights into larger human domains. Though critics have attributed fundamental errors to him, claiming that he misinterpreted the sexually repressed mores of turn-of-the-century Vienna as universal characteristics, his champions, in contrast, have argued that he uncovered hidden fundamentals at the core of human nature.

Freud discovered the motive force of individual behavior in the psyche, that is, the internal mental life of a person. In order to comprehend the function of this governing mechanism, he divided the mind into two parts, the conscious and the unconscious. The former, situated in the brain, produced deliberate, calculated thoughts, resulting in intentional acts to achieve designated goals and purposes. The latter, more remote and inaccessible by its very nature, lacked any awareness of itself but contained a resolution to the entire mystery of human motivation.

To make possible an understanding of an otherwise impenetrable phenomenon within the unconscious, Freud posited the existence of three functions. First, the *id*, the oldest of the psychical provinces, consisted of inherited instincts and contained a cauldron of consuming drives, lusts, desires, and cravings, all of which sought expression in forms unknown to the person possessing them. Second, the *ego* mediated between the demands of the id and the realities of the external world. To an extent, it defined the available range of possible forms of satisfaction, usually within the context of seeking after pleasure and avoiding pain. The third, the *superego*, functions as the conscience, deriving authority from mothers, fathers, and other such sources. More specifically, it perpetuated the experiences of childhood by prolonging into adulthood conceptions of right and wrong derived from "the personalities of the actual parents" and from "the family, racial, and national traditions handed on through them, as well as the demands of the immediate social milieu which they represent." As Freud further explained, "The id and the super-ego have one thing in common: they both represent the influence of the past—the id the influence of heredity, the super-ego the influence, essentially, of what is taken over from other people—whereas the ego is principally determined by the individual's own experience that is by accidental and contemporary events."[10]

The interaction and competition among these three components accounted for the unconscious mental life of all persons. Freud ranked the experiences of childhood as central. The relationships with parents and siblings and other such events, often long forgotten but still stored away in the recesses of the psyche, determined adult behavior in ways usually unrecognized by the human actor. Mild disturbances, obsessions, compulsions, and the like, called *neuroses*, required treatment through psychoanalysis, a therapeutic technique administered by a trained practitioner to make the patient conscious of hitherto unconscious psychical activity. Through the ensuing confrontation between the known and the unknown, a resolution of the remembered events with the unconscious traces should result in a cure. For drastically disarranged mental states called *psychoses*, Freud had more doubts about the possibilities of effecting much improvement.

Many of Freud's favorite phrases and ideas have become part of the jargon of the twentieth century. These include repression, projection, wish fulfillment, the analysis of dreams, the Freudian slip, and the Oedipus complex. Indeed, his emphasis on human sexuality as the source of the libidinal energy driving human beings has passed into current folklore. In contrast, his speculative writings on historical subjects have attracted less attention but at the same time have spurred a consuming interest among specialists who hope for deeper levels of understanding through the use of psychoanalytical history.

Freud's books, *Totem and Taboo* (1912), *Civilization and Its Discontents* (1930), and *Moses and Monotheism* (1939), set forth suggestive models. Each concerned an analysis of psychical events derived from clinical observations and people's relationships with the external world. As Freud explained, he wanted to study "the interactions between human nature, cultural development and the precipitates of primeval experiences." Religion figured prominently in these considerations and reflected "the dynamic conflicts between the ego, the id, and the super-ego, which psychoanalysis studies in the individual."

In *Totem and Taboo,* Freud combined some of the theoretical reflections of Charles Darwin with his own clinical observations. Freud borrowed a hypothesis holding that human beings originally lived in small hordes, each under the absolute rule of an older male who took all the females for himself and brutalized and killed the younger men, including his own sons. Such patriarchal oppression came to an end when the sons collectively rose in rebellion, destroyed the father-tyrant, and consumed his flesh. Consequently, the young males constituted a totemistic brother clan in which taboos forbade sexual contact with women within the group in favor of exogamy. Moreover, collective ambivalence over the killing of the father resulted in the adoption of a totem. Usually an animal, it stood for the clan's male ancestor, now transformed into a spirit protector. The males would allow no one to hurt it, except in a periodic ritual when the clan feasted upon the creature. According to Freud, "it was the solemn repetition of the father-murder in which social order, moral laws, and religion had their beginnings." For Freud, the actuality of any such event held little consequence. Whether real or fantasy, the psychic impulse to kill the father would have had the same outcome.

Similar characteristics marked *Civilization and Its Discontents* and *Moses and Monotheism.* In the former, Freud engaged in the speculative philosophy of history by musing about the direction of historical movement, particularly the transition from the religious to the scientific stage in human existence. Though ethnically Jewish, Freud never embraced the religious traditions of his heritage and, indeed, subjected them to merciless criticism. All religions he classified as mass delusions, unhappy and misguided efforts to substitute a wish fulfillment for an unbearable reality. In this work, he called upon human beings to give up childish responses and stoically face the truth. In *Moses and Monotheism,* he elaborated upon a related theme, claiming provocatively that Moses, actually an Egyptian, "chose" the Jews, led them out of bondage, and shaped them into a holy nation.

But the Jews, reacting against the Mosaic laws, murdered their leader and thereby reenacted the tribal horde experience with similar consequences, except in this instance a monotheistic conception of deity replaced the totem.

Such inferences outraged orthodox thinkers and have retained the capacity to disturb. Indeed, an animated controversy has developed, with Freud's champions on one side insisting that psychoanalytical history can arrive at more profound appraisals of human behavior and critics on the other rejecting his approach as a theory, neither proven nor provable. Perhaps most tellingly, the skeptics have depicted the techniques of Freud and his disciples primarily as therapies for which the only test of truth is practical: Does the patient get any better? If so, the practitioner has chosen the proper means of treatment and has arrived at a kind of truth. Unhappily, the historians employing psychoanalytical methods in their studies of dead people have no such means of verification and often have to indulge in speculative ruminations. Whether their inferential leaps illuminate the subject or obscure it remains an issue under debate.

In conclusion, a final example will illustrate the persistence of fundamental issues in discussions of speculative philosophy of history. In the United States during the 1940s, Reinhold Niebuhr attained a formidable rank as a theologian, philosopher, and political commentator. A "neo-orthodox" Protestant in his religious commitments, Niebuhr set forth new versions of the Christian view but operated steadfastly within the larger traditions of St. Augustine.

For Niebuhr, neither the classical nor the modern secular renditions of philosophy of history held much merit. The Greek cyclical idea deprived history of meaning by denying the significance of particular events. By submerging them in recurring patterns, according to Niebuhr, the Greeks denied to themselves the capacity to act creatively in particular instances and sought to escape into an abstract world of pure thought, thereby transcending history altogether. In contrary fashion, the Western linear and progressive construction of history put undue faith in the creative powers of human beings and found in history itself the means of attaining desirable goals, such as controlling nature, advancing human well-being, and democratizing society. In other words, the very course of historical development in itself would result in human betterment through the enhancement of freedom and good.

Because the modern approach found meaning in the details of historical existence, Niebuhr held it in higher regard than the classical, but he also believed that it suffered from a serious error by assuming a necessary connection between the growth of human freedom and good. For Niebuhr, no such relationship had ever existed. Indeed, to the contrary, the growth of human freedom and power simply "enlarges the scope of human problems" by giving greater opportunity for the expression of "egotistic desires and impulses." As examples, he noted:

> Modern industrial society dissolved ancient forms of political authoritarianism; but the tyrannies which grew on its soil proved more brutal and vexatious than the old ones. The inequalities rooted in landed property were levelled. But the more dynamic inequalities of a technical society became more perilous to the community than the more static forms of uneven power. The achievement of individual liberty was one of the genuine advances of bourgeois society. But this society also created atomic individuals, who, freed of the disciplines of the older organic communities, were lost in the mass; and became the prey of demagogues and charlatans who transmuted their individual anxieties and resentments into collective political power of demonic fury.[11]

Such views so typical of Niebuhr showed his taste for irony and paradox. Things seldom have turned out as people intended. Nevertheless, according to him, Christian conceptions of history guarded against naively optimistic expectations by espousing a more realistic and valid understanding of human nature. Christians knew the reality of original sin. This condition meant that, in the course of time, human beings could neither achieve their purposes consistently nor utilize their freedom and power to attain good. Nevertheless, Niebuhr insisted that the sovereignty of God presided over the whole of the human experience. As Niebuhr put it, "All historical destinies are under the dominion of a single divine sovereignty," which provides a "general frame of meaning for historical events." Moreover, Niebuhr denied that either reason or evidence could confirm such a claim. Only an affirmation of the Christian faith could result in the certainty that "history is potentially and ultimately one story."

Niebuhr strove to work out the implications of his position in two important works during the 1940s, *The Nature and Destiny of Man* and *Faith and History*. These stood as Christian rejections of modern secularists, such as Marx and Freud, and reduced the ancient debate to its stark essentials. Niebuhr insisted on meaning in history but found the ultimate source of meaning outside of history. Similarly, by rejecting the feasibility of rational or empirical demonstration, he removed the arbiter of debate from history to theology. Faith would have to decide. By such means, he closed the circle with St. Augustine.

RECOMMENDED READINGS

A useful compilation is available in Ronald H. Nash, ed., *Ideas of History*, Vol. 1: *Speculative Approaches to History* (New York: E. P. Dutton, 1969). Bruce Mazlish's *The Riddle of History: The Great Speculators from Vico to Freud* (New York: Minerva Press, 1966), provides good introductory essays. Additional commentary exists in Frank E. Manuel's *Shapes of Philosophical History* (Palo Alto: Stanford University Press, 1965); Karl Löwith's *Meaning in History: The Theological Implications of Philosophy of History* (Chicago: University of Chicago Press, 1949); and Peter Munz's *The Shapes of Time: A New Look at the Philosophy of History* (Middletown, CT: Wesleyan University Press, 1977). In *The Poverty of Historicism* (New York: Harper and Row, 1957), Karl R. Popper argues against the possibility of predicting the future. Introductions to Marx include David McClellan's *Karl Marx: His Life and Thought* (New York: Harper and Row, 1973); M. M. Bober's *Karl Marx's Interpretation of History*, 2nd ed. rev. (New York: W. W. Norton, 1965); Melvin Miller Rader's *Marx's Interpretation of History* (New York: Oxford University Press, 1979); and Gerald Allan Cohen's *Karl Marx's Theory of History: A Defense* (Princeton, NJ: Princeton University Press, 1978). *Telling the Truth about History* (New York: W. W. Norton, 1994) by Joyce Appleby, Lynn Hunt, and Margaret Jacob, contains a series of fine essays concerned with the emergence of modern historical consciousness.

Useful specialized works appear in Isaiah Berlin's *Vico and Herder: Two Studies in the History of Ideas* (New York: Viking Press, 1976); Mark Lilla's *G. B. Vico: The Making of an Anti-Modern* (Cambridge, MA: Harvard University Press, 1993); William A. Galston's *Kant and the Problem of History* (Chicago: University of Chicago Press, 1975); and Burleigh Taylor Wilkins's *Hegel's Philosophy of History* (Ithaca, NY: Cornell University Press, 1974). *The New Psychohistory* (New York: Psychohistory Press, 1975), ed. Lloyd de Mause, gives a ringing defense of this approach. More critical works by Jacques Barzun, *Clio and the Doctors: Psycho-History, Quanto-History and History* (Chicago: University of Chicago Press, 1974); and David E. Stannard, *Shrinking History: On Freud and the Failure of Psychohistory* (New York: Oxford University Press, 1980), raise important questions. Some compelling answers in Freud's defense appear in Peter Gay, *Freud for Historians* (New York: Oxford University Press, 1985). Freud's own book, *An Outline of Psycho-Analysis*, rev. ed., trans. James Strachey (New York: W. W. Norton, 1969), provides a resume of his thought. *The Irony of American History* (New York: Charles Scribner's Sons, 1952) by Reinhold Niebuhr sets forth some of the main themes.

Biographical works of special significance in addressing these topics include Richard Wightman Fox, *Reinhold Niebuhr: A Biography* (New York: Pantheon Books, 1985); Peter Gay, *Freud: A Life for Our Time* (New York: W. W. Norton, 1988); and William H. McNeil, *Arnold J. Toynbee: A Life* (New York: Oxford University Press, 1989).

ENDNOTES

1. Quoted in Bruce Mazlish, *The Riddle of History: The Great Speculators from Vico to Freud* (New York: Minerva Press, 1966), 38. See also *The New Science of Giambattista Vico*, revised translation of the third edition (1744), trans. Thomas Goddard Bergin and Max Harold Fisch (Ithaca, NY: Cornell University Press, 1968), 335–51.
2. Mazlish, *Riddle of History*, 90.
3. Ronald H. Nash, ed., *Ideas of History*, Vol. 1: *Speculative Approaches to History* (New York: E. P. Dutton, 1969), 61.
4. Nash, ed., *Ideas of History*, Vol. 2, 54.
5. Karl Marx, *The Communist Manifesto* (Chicago: Henry Regnery Co., 1954), 13–15.
6. Quoted in Mazlish, *Riddle of History*, 336; Oswald Spengler, *The Decline of the West*, abr. Helmut Werner (New York: Modern Library, 1962), 73–74.
7. Mazlish, *Riddle of History*, 320.
8. Arnold J. Toynbee, *A Study of History*, Vol. 2, abr. D. C. Somervell (New York: Oxford University Press, 1957), 357–58.
9. Arnold J. Toynbee,*Study of History*, 589.
10. Sigmund Freud, *An Outline of Psychoanalysis*, trans. James Strachey (New York: W. W. Norton, 1949), 16–17.
11. Reinhold Neibuhr, *Faith and History* (New York: Charles Scribner's Sons, 1949). Copyright renewed 1977 Ursula M. Neibuhr. Reprinted with permission of Charles Scribner's Sons.

5

PHILOSOPHY OF HISTORY: ANALYTICAL APPROACHES

The development of analytical or critical philosophy of history in the twentieth century has reflected a different set of concerns. This branch of intellectual inquiry has addressed issues in methodology and epistemology, particularly the crucial question: On what grounds can historians demonstrate that they know what they claim? The verifiability of historical knowledge comes under review. In this discussion, one kind of criterion measures the logic, rigor, and techniques of history against the prevailing forms in the natural sciences. Other issues include the formal requirements of an explanation, the meaning of causation, and the role of objectivity. Such matters have posed persistent problems and have elicited an ongoing debate. They have vital significance in comprehending the theoretical dimensions of the discipline.

The main lines of division go back to the seventeenth and eighteenth centuries, when Francis Bacon, René Descartes, and other scientists tried to establish more reliable means for studying the natural world. They and their successors favored mathematical formulations for testing and expressing their findings; they also liked high levels of generality by which to affirm statements of invariable relationship, or recurring uniformities and regularities among phenomena. Such statements took the following form. Whenever some combination of prior conditions existed in a particular instance, then a certain and predictable kind of outcome necessarily would follow. To utilize an example from nature, whenever fire heated water to the proper temperature and in the right circumstances, then steam would surely come about as a consequence.

Although the actual statements of invariable relationship became more intricate as the problems under observation grew more complex, the formal logical structure underlying them remained constant. For scientists, the greater extent to which they could express them in mathematical terms, the better. Ordinarily, formal logic connected the anterior or preceding conditions to the observable outcome by means of affirming a general empirical law. It said simply that, after repeated verifications through experimentation, whenever those kinds of conditions existed, the same outcome or consequence would take place. Put crudely in categories more congenial to historians, the invocation of a general law meant that, given the same causes, similar effects probably would occur.

Giambattista Vico in the eighteenth century repudiated such methods as inappropriate to historical studies, but the ascendancy of scientific models overwhelmed his objections. Some scholars dogmatically asserted that all forms of knowledge must conform to the methods and techniques of natural science or else forfeit any claim to the status of knowledge. Presumably inferior kinds of inquiry, those less demanding in logical form or less mathematical in orientation, would have to measure up against the dictates of "the hard sciences" or suffer disparagement as pseudoscience. For serious students of human affairs, the dilemma left open two courses of action. They could comply with the demand to emulate the natural sciences and seek to present their findings as general statements of invariable relationship. Such endeavors would lead to the development of the social sciences. Alternatively, they could insist on the propriety and integrity of the traditional methods and techniques within their own fields of study, disclaiming any need to adhere to the models of the natural sciences. Those in the latter camp sometimes depicted history as *sui generis*, that is, a class of learning unto itself.

A modern version of the debate appears in a book by Robert William Fogel and G.R. Elton entitled *Which Road to the Past? Two Views of History* (1983). It distinguished between "scientific" and "traditional" history with Fogel, an economic historian, championing the former, and Elton, an authority on Tudor England, the latter. As friendly intellectual rivals, neither scholar wished to disenfranchise the other as the possessor of a valid form of knowledge. Nevertheless, they favor distinctive versions. Fogel argues for the utility of social scientific models and mathematical formulations as a way to obtain general truths about the past. Elton wants historians to examine the existing evidence without preconceptions and then establish rational judgments about what it means.

Historically the controversy achieved special prominence in the middle of the nineteenth century with the advent of positivism. Primarily the work of Frenchman Auguste Comte but subsequently embraced by others such as John Stuart Mill, this body of thought sought to transform the study of human affairs into a systematic inquiry by endorsing the techniques of natural science. Rather than focus on unique or individual events, positivists concentrated on uniformities and similarities in the course of human affairs and then located the invariable relationships linking the same kinds of experiences. Rather than study the French Revolution, they would investigate the phenomenon of revolution while presuming the existence of general laws governing the outcomes of activity in the human world. While following the example of natural scientists, they put their trust in their own intellectual capabilities to find such laws.

The works of Auguste Comte gave rise to sociology and established the essentials in ten mighty volumes, *Cours de philosophie positive* (six volumes, 1830–42) and *Système de politique positive* (four volumes, 1851–54). To an extent, Comte's philosophy grew from his personal experiences, some of them a bit bizarre. Indeed, he obtained central insights leading to the Law of the Three Stages, a fundamental tenet, while suffering one of his periodic bouts with madness. The victim of an unhappy home life as a child, Comte fled to study mathematics at the École Polytechnique in Paris, abandoned Roman Catholicism, and for a time came under the influence of the French utopian socialist Henri de Saint-Simon. Though degrees of instability and eccentricity always marked Comte's personal life and sometimes found expression in unique forms of religiosity, for example, his commitment to a religion of humanity, he possessed the intellectual means to set forth an entire philosophical system called *positivism*.

Comte began with a trinitarian division, claiming as a basic premise that the human mind had developed historically through three stages. Straightforwardly Eurocentric, he focused his attention on the "vanguard of the human race," by which he meant the inhabitants of Italy, France, England, Germany, and Spain. He also preferred a high level of abstraction, espousing a wish to employ history, except for reasons of practicality, "without the names of men, or even of nations." Historian Bruce Mazlish explains this "dehumanization of history" as a result of Comte's determination to mimic the generalizing capabilities of the sciences. He ranked them in ascending order of difficulty, beginning with mathematics, a logical tool, followed by astronomy, physics, chemistry, physiology (biology), and at the pinnacle sociology.[1]

According to the Law of the Three Stages, Comte showed how the evolution of the human mind took place. In each body of knowledge, affirmations about reality progressed from the theological stage through the metaphysical stage to the positive stage. In the first, human beings saw the world as controlled by wills independent of their own but subject to propitiation or manipulation by prayer or magic. During the second, abstract forces, such as the requirements of nature or the will of the people, governed all things, and in the third, the positive and final stage, an understanding of the invariable relationships among phenomena would explain reality.

Echoing Vico and other predecessors, Comte also presumed holistic relationships, affirming that each mental stage corresponded with other kinds of intellectual and institutional developments. The theological phase coexisted with military life and primitive slavery, the metaphysical with lawyers and attempts at creating governments based on law, and the positive with industrialism. Comte's confusingly complicated efforts at refinement and elaboration allowed these categories to overlap, so that mathematics, the simplest form of knowledge, could achieve positive status in the otherwise theological age. But sociology, the most complex of all as the science of human beings, could attain this position only when all other forms of learning had also progressed to such a rank.

In the positive stage, no need would exist to indulge in idle speculation over first or final causes. Instead, using positivist principles, historians would concentrate on knowable subjects and the elucidation of lawlike regularities that affirmed invariable relationships among phenomena. These in turn would not depend upon theological or metaphysical presumptions but upon empirical observations of the real world. Once advanced to its highest form, the positivist philosophy would establish the basis for a new human science, sociology, the application of which would promote understanding of the laws governing human behavior and consequently new certainties over how best to calculate the probable outcomes of deliberate human acts.

Positivist philosophy generated strenuously adverse reactions. Usually called "idealist" in this debate, this school of thought took form around the writings of Wilhelm Dilthey, a German, Benedetto Croce, an Italian, and Robin G. Collingwood, an Englishman. For them, the analogy based on natural science had no validity, because history required different conceptual apparatus. Late in the nineteenth century, Dilthey distinguished between the natural sciences (*Naturwissenschaften*) on the one hand and the human sciences (*Geisteswissenschaften*) on the other. The practice of each called for distinctive methodologies, because the former sought regularities and uniformities in nature, while the latter dealt with unique, specific, and unrepeatable events outside of nature. For him, the difference between the general and the particular meant everything.

In the twentieth century, Croce, an important Italian intellectual, and Collingwood, an Oxford philosopher, historian, and archeologist, elaborated on similar conceptions of history. Croce emphasized the fact that historians existed in the present. For their studies to take on vitality and meaning, they must make the past come alive by rethinking it in their own minds. For this reason, Croce concluded, "all history is contemporary history." Collingwood set forth the fullest, most enduring exposition of the idealist position. His book, *The Idea of History*, published posthumously after his death in 1943 at age fifty-two still ranks among the most significant books on the philosophy of history ever published in English.

Collingwood described history as "the science of human nature," the aim of which promoted "self-knowledge." For him, the deceptive simplicity of this statement meant that the proper object of historical study focused on the human mind, or more properly the activities of the human mind, and that the appropriate means of investigation entailed "the methods of history." Historians learned about the mind by comprehending what the mind has done. Collingwood then discussed the disparity between the methods of the natural sciences and the human sciences and explained why the former had no analogous relationships with the latter. "The historian, investigating any event in the past, makes a distinction between what may be called the outside and the inside of an event." With these words, he established the crux of his message.

By the "outside of an event," Collingwood meant "everything belonging to it which can be described in terms of bodies and their movements: the passage of Caesar, accompanied by certain men, across a river called the Rubicon at one date, or the spilling of his blood on the floor of the senate-house at another." By "the inside of an event," he referred to that "which can only be described in terms of thought: Caesar's defiance of Republican law, or the clash of constitutional policy between himself and his assassins." To highlight the difference, Collingwood conceded that "the historian is never concerned with either of these to the exclusion of the other." As he explained, the work of the historian "may begin by discovering the outside of an event, but it can never end there; he must always remember that the event was an action, and that his main task is to think himself into this action, to discern the thought of his agent."

Collingwood then set forth another thesis. "In the case of nature, this distinction between the outside and the inside of an event does not arise." He stated, "The events of nature are merely events, not the acts of agents whose thought the scientist endeavors to trace." What takes place in nature manifests no inner life. "To the scientist, nature is always, and merely, a 'phenomenon' . . . a spectacle presented to his intelligent observation." For the historian, in contrast, "the events of history are never mere phenomena, never mere spectacles for contemplation, but things which the historian looks, not at, but through, to discern the thought within them."

Collingwood then summarized his point by putting it still another way. In seeking "the inside of events and detecting the thought which they express, the historian is doing something which the scientist need not and cannot do." Nevertheless, the methodological prescription for attaining this goal produced great problems. How shall the historian make certain of the thoughts acted out by human beings? According to Collingwood, "there is only one way in which it can be done: by re-thinking them in his own mind." Or, as he affirmed in another place, "The history of thought, and therefore all history, is the re-enactment of past thought in the historian's own mind." This creative and critical experience "reveals to the historian the powers of his own mind" and hence of all minds, resulting in a fuller appreciation of human nature as revealed by the mind while working on actual experience.[2]

For positivist critics, the idealist position partook of fantasy, mysticism, and self-deception. It called for explanations based on the operation of an unobservable entity called mind and required empathetic leaps into the heads of historical actors, all of which depended upon faith, not science. Under the criteria of the idealist alternative, the historian would know only when knowledge became knowable, and no other test would set forth a standard. For Comte's disciples, this premise lacked methodological integrity, defied verifiability through the use of evidence or observation, and belonged properly to the metaphysical stage of human development.

Collingwood and other idealists put down positivist charges on several grounds. First, in their view, they possessed methodological integrity, claiming that their approach, if carried out prudently and rigorously, allowed for verifiable insights into the workings of mind. Through the correct use of documentary evidence, that is, letters, diaries, and the like, the historian could make legitimate inferences. Second, they regarded the role of active, critical thought about the past as significant. Only by such means could they bring life into history. Collingwood denounced dullish recitations of mere facts based on earlier authorities as "scissors-and-paste history." Finally, Collingwood had no use for the positivist emphasis upon the need for generalization. As he remarked, "If, by historical thinking, we already understand how and why Napoleon established his ascendancy in Revolutionary France, nothing is added to our understanding of that process by the statement (however true) that similar things have happened elsewhere." To reinforce the point, he added, "It is only when the particular fact cannot be understood by itself that such statements are of value."[3]

The controversy between positivists and idealists became a dominant issue at mid century in discussions of philosophy of history and historical methodology. Divergent conceptions of explanation, causation, and objectivity underlie the debate and illustrate some of the complicated ramifications of historical thinking, thereby lending credence to the observation by philosopher W. H. Walsh that in truth "history is an altogether stranger and far more difficult discipline" than it is often taken to be.[4]

Another philosopher, Carl G. Hempel, established the main categories under discussion in 1942 with the publication of his seminal essay, "The Function of General Laws in History." In this presentation of the positivist case, Hempel argued that the explanatory forms of natural science indeed held true in the field of history. While defining a general law as "a statement of universal conditional form which is capable of being confirmed or disconfirmed by suitable empirical findings," he described the main function as an effort "to connect events in patterns which are usually referred to as explanation and prediction." A quotation from Hempel will indicate the line of reasoning:

> The explanation of the occurrence of an event of some specific kind at a certain place and time consists, as it is usually expressed, in indicating the causes or determining factors of E. Now the assertion that a set of events—say, of the kinds $C_1, C_2, \ldots, C_n$—have caused the event to be explained, amounts to the statement that, according to certain general laws, a set of events of the kinds mentioned is regularly accompanied by an event of kind E. Thus, the scientific explanation of the event in question consists of
> 1. a set of statements asserting the occurrence of events $C_1, \ldots, C_n$ at certain times and places,
> 2. a set of universal hypotheses, such that
>   a. the statements of both groups are reasonably well confirmed by empirical evidence,
>   b. from the two groups of statements the sentence asserting the occurrence of event E can be logically deduced.

The ensuing analysis, though complicated and difficult to follow upon first encounter, arrived at an emphatic conclusion: "The preceding considerations apply to explanation in history as well as in any other branch of empirical science." As Hempel affirmed, "Historical explanation, too, aims at showing that the event in question was not 'a matter of chance,' but was to be expected in view of certain antecedent or simultaneous conditions." Although in some instances "the universal hypotheses underlying a historical explanation are rather explicitly stated," Hempel conceded that most "fail to include an explicit statement of the general regularities they presuppose" because "they are tacitly taken for granted" or they lack "sufficient precision." As he noted, affirmations about the movement of Dust Bowl farmers to California in the 1930s have assumed a "universal hypothesis" to the effect that populations in times of hardship "will tend to migrate to regions which offer better living conditions." By omitting the authority of a general law, historians have employed what Hempel called "an explanation sketch."[5] Though incomplete in detail, it had to adhere, nevertheless, to the logical requirements of the explanation form.

The controversy has consumed analytically minded philosophers of history ever since. Dubbed "the covering-law model" by critic William Dray, the Hempel position called upon historians to explain specific events by subsuming them under a general proposition. But dissenters found little point in doing so and rejected such advice on several grounds. First, they noted that the actual practices of historians seldom conformed to Hempel's prescription. In their view, to follow it would render the entire exercise banal because of the absence of meaningful, agreed-upon general laws in the field of history. Either such generalizations do not exist or the lack of precision and specificity would deprive them of exactitude and explanatory power. Would anyone acquire a new and deeper understanding of the French Revolution by explaining that the French have always acted that way? Another criticism recalled Collingwood's critique. William Dray and others pointed out that the task of historians required them to make actions comprehensible within the context of the historical actors' own motives and aspirations. Once having elucidated the reasons for an act, the historian has nothing left to do.

In 1962, Hempel published another essay, seeking to meet the various attacks and to fend them off through tactical accommodations. This time he dealt directly with the actual writings of historians and allowed them some greater degree of flexibility. According to his array of definitions, the "probabilistic-statistical form" of explanation maintained "to the effect that if certain specified conditions are realized, then an occurrence of such and such a kind will come about with such and such a statistical probability." The "elliptic or partial" explanation sketch presupposed the existence of general laws but failed to invoke them explicitly, and the "genetic explanation" accounted for changing conditions in history by linking them systematically to earlier ones. But in each instance, Hempel still insisted upon holding historians to the requisites of what he now called "deductive-nomological explanation," asserting in good positivist fashion that "the nature of understanding . . . is basically the same in all areas of scientific inquiry." Indeed, he claimed to have demonstrated to his own satisfaction "the methodological unity of all empirical sciences."

The problem of defining causation in history also intrudes. The term "cause" has always produced perplexity. Historians usually have employed it in a commonsense fashion so that ordinary readers have access to their discussions. Nevertheless, ambiguous, imprecise usage of the term by historians has distressed logicians and philosophers. At least one authority, an Englishman, Michael Oakeshott, has recommended in favor of abandoning it altogether.

To illustrate some of the grounds for confusion, Aristotle once distinguished among four types of cause: the material, efficient, formal, and final. Among them, according to Ronald Nash, three have particular relevance to the study of history. An "efficient cause" refers to the prior events and conditions required for the occurrence of the main event, often by producing the needed energy. According to Nash, an observer might describe the cause of Abraham Lincoln's death as the bullet fired into his head by the assassin John Wilkes Booth. A "formal cause" accounts for an event through the location of "dispositional properties" needed to bring it about. A window might break because glass is brittle, or in Lincoln's case, death occurred because Booth as a Confederate sympathizer hated him. Last, a "final cause" accounts for an event by attributing it to the will or purpose of an agent. In this instance, Lincoln died because Booth wanted to get rid of him in hopes of obtaining more generous treatment of the defeated Confederacy.

Advocates of the positivist and idealist schools are also sharply divided over the question of cause in the study of history. The former must attach meaning to the term "cause" in the efficient sense as the most appropriate, that is, as a set of prior events and conditions. Moreover, as a kind of corollary, they usually conceived of cause as energy, based on a sort of mechanistic notion derived from physics. Just as the impact of the cue ball impels the eight ball into the side pocket in pool, so the combined effects of population pressures and land scarcities compelled people to move to the great American West. Idealists, in contrast, have understood the term in the sense of final cause. For them, it necessarily meant the will or intention of the historical actors. Purposeful action was the key. Once having ascertained Brutus's thoughts while stabbing Caesar, the historian could aspire to nothing else.

Still another difficulty has compounded the problem of cause. While discussing causation, analytical philosophers have often established distinctions between necessary and sufficient conditions in accounting for the course of human events. Necessary conditions involve probabilities. A statement of them refers to the minimum requirements necessary to allow an event to take place. The focus centers on likelihood rather than certainty. Sufficient conditions, in contrast, involve inevitabilities. A statement of them would amount to a guarantee that a certain outcome will result. Because historians usually debate the causes of big and complicated events, such as the fall of the Roman Empire or the onset of the First World War, they seldom can handle all the variables under consideration. As a result of the limitations of intellect, historians most often traffic only in necessary conditions. Their narratives, rightly understood, almost always ponder probabilities, almost never inevitabilities.

The last issue under discussion in this chapter is the nature of objectivity. Often described as the most important and the most difficult methodological problem facing historians, objectivity as traditionally conceived requires that scholars ignore personal bias to the extent possible while describing the subject under consideration as accurately as possible. Debate about the degree to which historians have attained this goal and can ever hope to do so has resulted in profound disparities. A study by Peter Novick, *That Noble Dream: The "Objectivity Question" and the American Historical Profession* (1988), explores the matter. Though the contours of the debate do not strictly follow the positivist–idealist cleavage, the two positions still suggest the magnitude of the disagreement.

The positivist argument once again would hold the historians to the standards of natural science by insisting that any other option will result in a diminution of rigor and believability. To demand anything less would disqualify history from the ranks of empirically based, scientific disciplines and relegate it to the status of pseudoscience, perhaps on a par with alchemy and phrenology. Such criteria presuppose laboratory techniques by which natural scientists seek to exclude variable factors and to exert maximum controls. Such procedures presume a large measure of repeatability; that is, anyone carrying out the experiment in the same way and under the same conditions ought to arrive at the same findings and conclusions.

For historians, this conception of objectivity presents two immediate obstacles. First, historians do not work in laboratories and can neither exclude confusing variables nor control other conditions. For obvious reasons, their objects of study compel different approaches. Moreover, the idea of repeatability has less bearing. Indeed, a reverse kind of consideration has come into play. Among "hard scientists," history and other "soft" sciences in human studies are sometimes viewed as suspect because scholars have difficulty arriving at solid agreements and confirming one another's findings. According to this stereotype, if ten historians scrutinized the same bodies of evidence, they probably would arrive at ten different versions of meaning and significance.

Even so, what critics might regard as disorder and disarray, historians would view as a sign of intellectual vitality. The body of literature on almost any historical subject takes the form of an ongoing debate.

Whether this aversion to consensus has reduced history to the status of pseudoscience has precipitated even more dissension. Some historians, inclined toward a relativist view, have argued that the measure of objectivity in history will always differ from that in natural science. After all, historians traditionally have investigated all sorts of human matters charged with passion and emotion. By the very nature of the subject, history tends to divide scholars and to set them at odds. It is one thing to study pulleys and inclined planes, quite another Second World War and the Holocaust. Moreover, individual historians cannot always achieve detachment or indifference. Each one arguably displays a bias through the mere choice of a subject for study, perhaps the origin of a social problem, and then compounds the difficulty by bringing other partialities to it derived from culture, class, race, gender, religion, or some other form of personal identification. To be sure, personal preferences need not represent gross bigotry. Nevertheless, they may lead to value judgments in the narratives and affect evaluative methods. Another problem resides in the historian's practice of choosing specific facts for inclusion while excluding others. Because these are chosen from an already incomplete body of historical data, the chances of skewing the story in one way or another are enhanced even more.

Whatever the risk of personal bias, the dangers of writing history do not appreciably exceed those of natural science where similar hazards exist. Natural scientists also choose a subject for investigation, such as cancer research, and perhaps in this way betray a preference acquired from life experiences. They also draw conclusions based on less-than-total knowledge. Indeed, no academic discipline aspires to recreate reality but rather to obtain some insight into its essential nature. For such reasons, the epistemological predicaments of natural science run parallel in important respects with those of history.

Nevertheless, historians do operate under a singular disadvantage. As American historian Carl L. Becker observed, "In truth the actual past is gone; and the world of history is an intangible world, re-created in our minds."[6] In contrast with many forms of natural science, no actual object ever comes under observation. Instead, while using the remnants of the past, historians reconstruct history, employing statements of probability, not certainty, and subject always to the limitations of a point of view.

The angle of vision renders historical narratives intelligible. Without it, historical artifacts would make no sense, and historical narratives would follow no coherent line of development. True, historians do not always agree, but different versions of the same events do not necessarily result in intellectual incompatibility or error. Quite the contrary, divergent renditions may result in larger, complementary forms of understanding in which one enriches and animates the other from separate vantage points. Theoretically, the number of "true" stories historians can tell about the past is unlimited. Charles Beard, an American historian, always maintained that his work, an economic interpretation of the U.S. Constitution, in no way nullified political or ideological or institutional treatments. It merely added a new dimension.

Though the problem of objectivity no doubt will remain a source of perplexity and consternation, historian Paul K. Conkin has suggested a wise way of moderating the dilemma. While properly refusing to abandon conceptions of truth and believability in historical narratives, he argued that different standards of objectivity must apply than in the natural sciences. Historians must adhere to their own rules of fairness, reason, and logic while constructing their stories about the human past. In addition, they must support their claims with some kind of evidence as the basis for plausible and valid inferences. To the extent that they comply, the works of historians will fulfill the requirements of objectivity.[7]

Historians can sacrifice conceptions of objectivity only at their own risk. A most disturbing manifestation has come about in recent times. A crowd of self-proclaimed "historical revisionists" has gained an audience by insisting that the genocide directed against European Jewry during the Second World War never happened. These so-called Holocaust deniers depict claims of mass extermination as a gigantic hoax perpetrated by Zionists in support of the state of Israel. Organized into "the Institute for Historical Review," they have published their denials in the *Journal of Historical Review*, a means of presentation dressed up with the appearance of scholarly apparatus in order to make untruths seem believable. According to historian Deborah Lipstadt, a leading authority, such lies are the work of an unsavory group of pseudoscholars with pro-Nazi and anti-Semitic proclivities. None of them are professional historians. According to her powerful and distressing book *Denying the Holocaust: The Growing Assault on Truth and Memory*, the reality of the Holocaust is not debatable.[8] The catastrophe happened, and the proof exists. Yet gullible people in the United States and Europe have accepted the denial as plausible. Lipstadt calls upon historians as truth tellers to stand against this attempt at overturning reason and evidence. Epistemological integrity does count for something.

The discussion in this chapter has aimed not at resolving the theoretical issues in dispute in the study of history but rather at providing some guidance in following the main lines of debate and pointing out some of the methodological pitfalls. Upon serious encounter, such issues do not allow for facile assumptions about much of anything. The controversy over the positivist and idealist models has shaped the discussion, but the models do not imply the existence of two different kinds of reality. Rather, they suggest two different attempts at comprehending portions of the natural and the historical worlds. They also recall the distinction established by Sir Isaiah Berlin in an essay on Leo Tolstoy's philosophy of history. Berlin derived the essay's title, *The Hedgehog and the Fox*, from a line of poetry by Archilochus that said, "The fox knows many things, but the hedgehog knows one big thing."

Berlin believed that those words marked one of the deepest differences among writers and thinkers. As he explained in a kind of extended thesis statement:

> For there exists a great chasm between those, on the one side, who relate everything to a single central vision, one system less or more coherent or articulate, in terms of which they understand, think and feel—a single, universal, organizing principle in terms of which alone all that they are and say has significance—and, on the other side, those who pursue many ends, often unrelated and even contradictory, connected, if at all, only in some de facto way, for some psychological or physiological cause, related by no moral or aesthetic principle; these last lead lives, perform acts, and entertain ideas that are centrifugal rather than centripetal, their thought is scattered or diffused, moving on many levels, seizing upon the essence of a vast variety of experiences and objects for what they are in themselves without, consciously or unconsciously, seeking to fit them into or exclude them from, any one unchanging, all-embracing, sometimes self-contradictory and incomplete, at times fanatical, unitary inner vision.

Berlin noted, "The first kind of intellectual and artistic personality belongs to the hedgehogs, the second to the foxes." Without insisting upon any kind of rigid classification, he suggested that Dante belonged to the first category and Shakespeare to the second. Plato, Lucretius, Pascal, Hegel, Dostoevsky, Nietzsche, Ibsen, and Proust ranked as hedgehogs, and Herodotus, Aristotle, Montaigne, Erasmus, Moliere, Goethe, Pushkin, Balzac, and Joyce were foxes. His observations pointed toward something fundamental and widespread. If they held credence, then perhaps the very existence of the positivist–idealist dichotomy partook of the universal and expressed a distinctive facet of the workings of mind. If so, it may brook no resolution.[9]

RECOMMENDED READINGS

Useful compilations are contained in Ronald H. Nash, ed., *Ideas of History*, Vol. 2: *The Critical Philosophy of History* (New York: E. P. Dutton, 1969); Patrick Gardiner, ed., *Theories of History* (New York: Free Press, 1959); and William H. Dray, ed., *Philosophical Analysis and History* (New York: Harper and Row, 1966). William H. Dray, *Philosophy of History*, 2nd ed. (Englewood Cliffs, NJ: Prentice-Hall, 1993); W. H. Walsh, *Philosophy of History: An Introduction*, rev. ed. (New York: Harper and Row, 1967); and the segment by Paul K. Conkin in Conkin and Roland N. Stromberg, *The Heritage and Challenge of History* (New York: Dodd, Mead and Co., 1971), provide additional materials. Conkin's thoughts on objectivity are contained in Chapter 11. For a similar defense of conceptions of objectivity in history, see Chapter 7 in Joyce Appleby, Lynn Hunt, and Margaret Jacob, *Telling the Truth about History* (New York: W. W. Norton, 1994). The main scholarly journal in this area is *History and Theory: Studies in the Philosophy of History.*

The debate over "the covering law" figures prominently in Arthur C. Danto, *Analytical Philosophy of History* (Cambridge, MA: Harvard University Press, 1965); William Dray, *Laws and Explanation in History* (New York: Oxford University Press, 1957); Haskell Fain, *Between Philosophy and History: The Resurrection of Speculative Philosophy of History within the Analytic Tradition* (Princeton, NJ: Princeton University Press, 1970); Leon J. Goldstein, *Historical Knowing* (Austin: University of Texas Press, 1976); Oscar Handlin, *Truth in History* (Cambridge, MA: Belknap Press of Harvard University Press, 1979); J. H. Hexter, *Doing History* (Bloomington: Indiana University Press, 1971); and Morton White, *Foundations of Historical Knowledge* (New York: Harper and Row, 1965). The two essays by Carl G. Hempel are reprinted in Nash and Gardiner. Representative writings by Carl Becker and

Charles Beard are also in Nash. The emergence of an alternate view is examined by Georg G. Iggers, *The German Conception of History: The National Tradition of Historical Thought from Herder to the Present* (Middletown, CT: Wesleyan University Press, 1968). The premier statement of the "idealist" position, of course, is R. G. Collingwood, *The Idea of History* (New York: Oxford University Press, 1956). The concluding consideration comes from Isaiah Berlin, *The Hedgehog and the Fox* (New York: Mentor, 1957).

Important contributions to the literature include Robert William Fogel and G.R. Elton, *Which Road to the Past? Two Views of History* (New Haven, CT: Yale University Press, 1983); and Peter Novick, *That Noble Dream: The "Objectivity Question" and the American Historical Profession* (New York: Cambridge University Press, 1988). John Tosh, *The Pursuit of History: Aims, Methods, and New Directions in the Study of Modern History*, 2nd ed. (London: Longman, 1991), covers many of the issues under review in this chapter. Deborah Lipstadt's *Denying the Holocaust: The Growing Assault on Truth and Memory* (New York: Free Press, 1993) presents a dismaying account of a monstrous misuse of history. Additional considerations of related matters appear in Michael Shermer and Alex Grobman, *Denying History: Who Says the Holocaust Never Happened and Why They Say It?* (Berkeley: University of California Press, 2000); and Richard J. Evans, *Lying about Hitler: History, Holocaust, and the David Irving Trial* (New York: Basic Books, 2001).

ENDNOTES

1. Bruce Mazlish, *The Riddle of History: The Great Speculators from Vico to Freud* (New York: Minerva Press, 1966), 194–96.
2. R. G. Collingwood, *The Idea of History* (New York: Oxford University Press, 1956), 204–15.
3. Collingwood, *Idea of History*, 223.
4. Ronald H. Nash, ed., *Ideas of History*, Vol. 2: *The Critical Philosophy of History* (New York: E. P. Dutton, 1969), 240.
5. Carl G. Hempel, "The Function of General Laws in History," in *Theories of History*, ed. Patrick Gardiner (New York: Free Press, 1959), 344, 348–49. First published in *Journal of Philosophy*, 39 (15 January 1942), 36.
6. Ronald H. Nash, ed., *Ideas of History*, Vol. 2: *The Critical Philosophy of History* (New York: E. P. Dutton, 1969), 185.
7. Paul K. Conkin and Roland N. Stromberg, *The Heritage and Challenge of History* (New York: Dodd, Mead and Co., 1971), 211; Joyce Appleby, Lynn Hunt, and Margaret Jacob, *Telling the Truth about History* (New York: W. W. Norton, 1994), Chapter 7, also insists upon the importance of retaining conceptions of objectivity.
8. Deborah Lipstadt, *Denying the Holocaust: The Growing Assault on Truth and Memory* (New York: Free Press, 1993).
9. Isaiah Berlin, *The Hedgehog and the Fox: An Essay on Tolstoy's View of History* (New York: Mentor, 1957), 7–8.

6

PROFESSIONAL HISTORY
IN RECENT TIMES

The professionalization of history beginning in the middle of the nineteenth century produced profound changes in focus and direction and also inspired fierce struggles over purposes and methods. When historians first endorsed a conception of "scientific" history, they promoted detached objectivity while examining documentary evidence and seeking irrefutable truths. They emphasized assiduous research and stringent techniques. Their successors had less faith. Some doubted the accessibility of unquestionable verities and urged the acquisition of socially useful insights, emphasizing the importance of viewing the subject from different angles. Others looked for more inclusive, reliable methods and for deeper levels of understanding by extending inquiries beyond the political, military, and diplomatic activities of male elites and applying the social sciences. In recent times, champions of cultural anthropology, linguistic analysis, and literary criticism have explored the relevance of these disciplinary techniques to history. Such tendencies have generated mixed results. Though historical studies have become more precise and thorough, the preoccupations of professionalization have also promoted isolation and fragmentation. Because of pervasive specialization, common varieties of historical understanding broke down. In their place, pluralistic interpretations testify to the disparities of human experience.

In *Historiography: Ancient, Medieval and Modern*, historian Ernst Breisach discusses these changes while arguing that four main influences have shaped historical thinking since 1870: the impact of natural science, the process of industrialization, the emergence of mass culture, and shifting perceptions of a global world. According to Breisach, science, often regarded as the model of all knowledge, set profound epistemological problems before historians. Meanwhile, the disruptions brought about by the Industrial Revolution destroyed traditional understanding of cultural unity and historical continuity. Similarly, the concentration of rootless mass populations in urban regions and the subsequent threat of political destabilization by crowds of malcontents drew scholarly attention to the activities of nonelites. About the same time, the imperial triumph of the West over the rest of the world gave credibility to Eurocentric ideas of world history. Later, the collapse of this hegemony after the Second World War compelled conceptual revisions of such formulations. In combination, the effects shattered uniform pictures of the past and resulted in great divergences.

During the closing years of the nineteenth century, the so-called "hard" sciences acquired immense prestige for their capacity to produce demonstrable claims about reality and to develop reliable predictive devices. Students of human affairs, including historians, looked toward them as examples to emulate, but doing so posed enormous conceptual difficulties, chief among them, the distinction between the general and the particular. Allowing for exceptions such as astronomy, the sciences characteristically developed general statements about the natural world, while history concentrated on particularistic statements about human affairs. If historians mimicked the scientists, they might lose their distinctive identity. If universal principles and covering-law theories became the hallmarks, then history would have to undergo a transformation in the image of physics or chemistry or else would cease to exist as a legitimate form of knowledge.

The epistemological controversies reviewed earlier aligned positivists against idealists and sometimes set historians against one another. Though innovators invoked the social sciences in the quest for methodological reassurance and scientific exactitude, traditionalists resisted the allure of arguments by analogy, insisting that in their field the term "science" possessed a more restricted meaning. For them, methodological rigor required that they strip away unwarranted theological and philosophical assumptions, accumulate the evidence, and then scrutinize it coldly, analytically, and objectively without preconceptions. Practiced with rigor and detachment, history, as English historian J. B. Bury observed in 1903, would amount to a science, "no less and no more."[1]

Other historians, spurred on by the harsh circumstances of the industrial age, arrived at new understandings of the true forces shaping history by emphasizing the effects of dramatically jolting economic change. For them, abstract and idealistic conceptions of the universe defined in supernatural or metaphysical or rationalistic terms held less reality than the press of material conditions. According to the materialist view, economic struggle to earn a livelihood typified human behavior, and the pursuit of wealth functioned as a prime determinant. Karl Marx set forth his positions on these subjects in the middle of the nineteenth century, and, henceforth, both the Marxist and the non-Marxist varieties of history directed attention toward the organization of the productive system and the means by which people earned their living. Such pursuits turned into economic history.

The concentration of burgeoning masses in the cities also compelled notice and contributed to new kinds of social history. They focused on common, ordinary people. Though never completely anonymous in historical narratives, such persons, typically powerless, inconspicuous, and caught up in cycles of birth, labor, and death, occupied a subordinate place under dominant ruling male elites who controlled politics, diplomacy, and war. Indeed, the very historical records employed by historians—political, diplomatic, and military—restricted access to such human types. They showed up mainly in the announcements of birth and death. Though Marxist methods emphasized the reality of the class struggle throughout history, most nineteenth-century historians who wrote about "the people" had in mind collectivities of human beings who found their stories incorporated into the histories of their nations. In the twentieth century, historians turned their investigations to the development of group identities, particularly workers, peasants, racial and ethnic groups, women, and families, that is, historical actors who could not find their stories in traditional, national histories.

Finally, Western ascendancy over the rest of the world initially compelled self-congratulatory conceptions of universal or world history. Almost always ethnocentric, the various renditions, whether providential or secular, Christian or Marxist, characteristically took Western Europe as the model of historical development for all humanity and displayed scant sensitivity to the experiences of other peoples in other places. Oswald Spengler ranked as an exception. In

Eurocentric renditions, human differences appeared as deviances, and European standards became the norms, indeed, the hallmarks of civilization itself. In the nineteenth century, colonialism and imperialism in Asia, Africa, and the Middle East impressed Europeans not only as manifestations of a divinely ordained, civilizing mission in the barbarous regions but as irrefutable signs of their own intrinsic superiority, defined in social Darwinian terms as justification for their ascendancy over lesser peoples. In the United States, an ideological counterpart affirmed the doctrine of manifest destiny in various guises. Viewed in such terms, universal or world history became merely a projection of the European (or American) experience, part and parcel of a progressive thrust moving the inhabitants of the globe ever onward. In recent times, certain sociological and economic theories of "modernization" based on Western models, such as W. W. Rostow's *The Stages of Economic Growth: A Non-Communist Manifesto* (1960) incorporated vestiges of this theme, but in the rest of the world, such ideas forfeited credibility when the Europeans lost their dominance and their empires. As a consequence, Western scholars with interests in non-Western history had to start all over again, seeking new perspectives, categories, and methods for understanding the histories of non-European peoples on their own terms. New conceptions of global history and postcolonial studies have pursued such ends.

At the end of the nineteenth century, European historians took special interest in the continuities of historical experience. Focusing mainly on the institutional development of constitutional and legal systems, scholars explored questions of national identity and indulged in arcane discussions over its origins. These issues had patriotic implications. In Germany and France, medievalists such as Heinrich von Sybel and Fustel de Coulanges debated whether the primary influences shaping their countries had Frankish or Roman antecedents. In England, investigations revolved around constitutional history and the Whig interpretation underscoring the extension of liberty and the role of Parliament. Whether the modern English nation had its roots in ancient Anglo-Saxon or European practices became significant.

In the United States, similar preoccupations expressed national identity and pride. In the middle of the nineteenth century, George Bancroft and other "literary historians" rejoiced in the nation's birth and growth, seeing in the fledgling democracy indications of divine favor. Such conceptions of organic unity and supernatural direction broke down after the Civil War, the result of sectionalism, industrialization, urbanization, immigration, and class strife. Consequently, a new generation of university-trained historians in the 1880s and 1890s sought to harness more rigorous means of historical analysis. The creation of the American Historical Association in 1884 testified to their professional commitment.

Inspired by conceptions of scientific history, American historians followed the Europeans in their concern for institutional growth. Early renditions traced the lineage of American liberty to a Germanic heritage. Professor Herbert Baxter Adams presented this argument in his seminar at the Johns Hopkins University, locating the "germ" of later developments in the misty Teutonic forests. His idea could not withstand scholarly scrutiny and dissolved under pressure from various sources, including the "imperial school" of colonial history. Scholars such as Herbert L. Osgood, George Louis Beer, and Charles McLean Andrews located the roots of American republicanism not in German villages but in English legacies and the colonial experience in the New World.

The dislocations of the age called forth the Progressive reform movement featuring new conventions in academic scholarship, particularly in law, philosophy, social science, and history. Seeking to promote "progress" through conscious planning, historians during the Progressive era developed what became known as the "New History." As skeptical iconoclasts, the "new historians" regarded high-blown, idealistic rhetoric as subterfuge of self-interest. An early version appeared in the works of Frederick Jackson Turner. In 1893, he read before the American Historical Association a paper on the significance of the frontier in American history. His seminal idea, "the frontier thesis," retained influence within the profession for over half a century and shifted the focus of study in U.S. history. First, Turner repudiated the view of Herbert Baxter Adams, his teacher who claimed that American institutions had germinated in the Teutonic woods. Turner saw liberty, democracy, and individualism as homegrown traits, the products of the frontier experience. Second, he focused attention away from New England toward the West, where successive acts of settlement had engendered the laudable qualities of which he spoke. Elusive and poetic, Turner's writings never made clear whether the author understood the frontier as a place, a process, or a state of mind. Nevertheless, the Turner thesis captivated historians, because it accounted for American uniqueness and put ordinary white people, the settlers, at the center of things. It had less to offer native peoples and other victims of westward expansion.

Another historian who shaped the consciousness of the time, Charles Austin Beard, developed an economic interpretation of U.S. history. More indebted to James Madison and *The Federalist Papers* than to Karl Marx, Beard, an activist and reformer, directed attention to the founding fathers. In 1913, the publication of *An Economic Interpretation of the Constitution* set forth heretical views. While emphasizing the impact of class conflict, Beard disparaged the supposed effects of altruistic impulses and providential design by underscoring the complex interplay of material concerns. Indeed, he portrayed a contest between a popular party based on paper money and agrarian preoccupations and a conservative party founded on urban, financial, mercantile, and personal property interests. For Beard, the adoption of the Constitution, a triumph for the latter, really amounted to a counterrevolution against the alleged democratic excesses under the Articles of Confederation. In a later work entitled *The Rise of American Civilization*, first published in 1934, Beard and his collaborator, his wife Mary, accentuated economic causes while arguing that the selfish business classes had consistently opposed the common good.

Especially poignant during the Great Depression, such themes figured prominently in the Progressive school of historiography in the United States. During these years of political and economic upheaval, Progressive historians retained hopes for the future and expressed a cherished regard for democratic traditions out of concern for maintaining them in a violent industrial age. Through the mechanisms of social science, rationality, cooperation, and planning, they hoped to retain the best of the past in the years to come by means of reform.

The major works by Progressive historians highlighted conflict in the American experience, defined either in class or in sectional terms. In a study of the origins of the American Revolution, *A History of Political Parties in the Province of New York, 1768–1776* (1909), Carl L. Becker described a struggle not only against English authority but against the colonial oligarchy which possessed of monopolistic power and wealth. As Becker noted, the issue became a question not only of home rule but also who should rule at home. The sectional emphasis, to an extent inspired by Frederick Jackson Turner, gave a conspicuous role to competition among regions, each with distinctive geographic, economic, political, and social characteristics. When presented in this way, U.S. history turned into a story of rivalry among the East, the South, and the West.

While Turner concentrated on the frontier regions and inspired debate over his thesis for years, other scholars found inspiration in other localities and issues. The works of Vernon Parrington, Perry Miller, and Samuel Eliot Morison illuminated New England traditions, especially the Puritan heritage. The South, in spite of its "peculiar institution" of slavery, provoked sympathetic investigations of white elites by William A. Dunning and a cluster of historians around him. The Civil War figured as a central event for Progressive historians. Although Beard treated this struggle in economic terms—a second American Revolution resulting in the dominance of the industrial classes—his revisionist successors, notably James G. Randall in *The Civil War and Reconstruction* (1937), explained the war as the consequence of human folly, the catastrophic work of "a blundering generation." For Civil War scholars, the questions of causation and inevitability—that is, whether the fighting was avoidable or not—took on fundamental significance.

Paradoxically, Progressive historians displayed scant interest in scrutinizing race and gender relations in the United States and left that writing to others. Consequently, some narratives incorporated negative racial assumptions. Ulrich B. Phillips understood slavery as a way of coping with an "inferior" race. In contrast, black historians, notably W. E. B. Du Bois and Carter G. Woodson, both educated at Harvard University, engaged in political and intellectual struggles during their long careers to enhance the understanding and the status of black people. Du Bois participated in founding the National Association for the Advancement of Colored People (NAACP) and the *Journal of Negro History*.

Though neglectful of some issues, Progressive historians tried to write useful history while elucidating the nature of contemporary social issues. Indeed, their advocacy of political causes set some of them at odds with the standards of scientific history and raised questions about the attainability of the objective truth. For Carl Becker and Charles Beard, "that noble dream," in Beard's words, would always elude fulfillment. For Becker and Beard, public utility, not merely accuracy, should guide the construction of historical narratives. When Beard spoke dubiously of objectivity before the American Historical Association in 1935, he raised a storm over his dangerous flirtation with the doctrine of relativism. If the criterion of objectivity could not hold, then historians could never assure themselves that they knew anything at all. The issue is addressed in Peter Novick's book *That Noble Dream: The "Objectivity Question" and the American Historical Profession* (1988).

Doubt and uncertainty assailed historians all over the world during the decade of the Great Depression, although in some countries totalitarian renditions provided illusions of certainty. In Italy, fascist accounts, exalting the leadership principle, identified Benito Mussolini as the manifestation of the national will but failed to give the same status to important Italian intellectuals. Benedetto Croce, a philosopher and historian, dissented from fascist orthodoxy, and Antonio Gramsci, a Marxist sociologist, paid for his opposition with his life. His letters from jail years after his death wielded an important influence on changing conceptions of cultural history. Similarly, in Germany the doctrines of National Socialism and the racism attached to them created havoc within the universities and resulted in purges of Jewish professors, sacrificing some of the best minds in that country. Nazi historiography functioned as propaganda by venerating German warriors, military power, and the authority of the state. Nazi legacies left future generations of German historians with the obligation of wrestling with the problems of guilt and responsibility.

In the Soviet Union, Marxism became the state ideology. Though traditionally much influenced by German notions of rigor and objectivity, Russian historians of bourgeois origin became suspect during the Stalin era, when the dictator intervened in academic disputes in efforts to ensure "correct" interpretations of history. As a consequence, Bolshevik doctrines became unassailable and the Russian Revolution an unquestioned anticipation of the future elsewhere. According to the orthodox view, the Soviet Union would assume leadership in bringing about the fulfillment of Marxist–Leninist prophecies and the establishment of world communism. For a time during the Second World War, called "the Great Patriotic War" in Russia, the desperation of this life-and-death struggle led to an emphasis on more traditional nationalism. Subsequently, the reappearance of the hard-line Stalinist history after the peace reaffirmed the hegemony of the official ideology not only within the Soviet Union but over "the people's republics" in Eastern Europe as well.

Elsewhere, Marxian scholars, removed from Stalin's authority, struggled with the intellectual puzzles of reconciling fact with theory and thought with practice. Among the members of the so-called Frankfurt school in Germany during the 1930s, critical thinkers repudiated simple-minded varieties of "vulgar" Marxism, that is, a dogmatic, unquestioning emphasis on economics, and urged a fuller appreciation of the diversity of influences shaping human behavior. Erich Fromm sought some form of amalgamation with psychoanalysis. During the Hitler years, the dispersion of the Frankfurt school to other countries introduced its principals (e.g., Herbert Marcuse) to the rigors of Anglo-Saxon empiricism and at the same time invigorated more conventional thinking outside Germany with exposure to sophisticated Marxian analysis.

French scholars also participated in the effort to obtain more comprehensive understanding of the human past. Led by Marc Bloch and Lucien Febvre, the founders in 1929 of the journal *Annales d'histoire économique et sociale*, the historians making up the *Annales* School rebelled against the prevailing forms of academic history. Rejecting the narrow emphasis on politics, war, and diplomacy, what Febvre disparaged as *histoire événementielle*, or event-oriented history, the *Annalistes* strove to grasp the many dimensions of human reality. As the historiographer Ernst Breisach explained, these French scholars envisioned a new, more complete history, inclusive of all aspects of human life. To achieve the aim, they developed a larger repertoire of investigative techniques, many derived from sociology, and called for extensive cooperation with "comrades and brothers" across all the social and human sciences. As Febvre expressed the goal, "Down with all barriers and labels!"[2]

Annaliste tenets triumphed among French historians after 1945. The group's journal resumed publication under a new title, *Annales: Economies, societés, civilisation*, and *Annaliste* scholars resumed their quest for more total history. Surprisingly, they seldom wrote explicitly about method and theory. As a Nazi prisoner before his execution, the famed medievalist and resistance fighter Marc Bloch composed *The Historian's Craft*, a modest methodological survey but hardly a manifesto.

Two traits figured conspicuously in their works. First, *Annaliste* scholars built upon a conception of collective consciousness. Termed *mentalité*, it focused on the mental and psychological characteristics of groups at specified times and places, thereby moving beyond exaggerated concerns with individuals. In this approach, the collectivity counted most in explanations leading to total history. Second, *Annaliste* historians employed a notion of the *longue durée*, that is, the long duration. As a conception of time, this term depicted the structural continuities intruding upon the course of historical change. The *longue durée* comprised the land, the sea, the climate, and the vegetation. These conditions represented stabilizing influences on the conduct of human affairs and impelled a slower pace or rhythm than the transitory events of politics, war, and diplomacy. They determined, moreover, the manner of life.

The best-known work by an *Annaliste* historian, Fernand Braudel's *The Mediterranean World in the Age of Philip II* first appeared in 1949. It set forth ambitious aims, seeking to encompass the totality of life in the region while focusing on the uniformities in the political, social, economic, intellectual, and geographic realms. Braudel's concern for continuities, the overarching structures of time, and the languid pace of change, and his efforts to develop conceptual unities, obtained many impressive results but, according to his critics, seldom achieved the desired level of integration. The sheer magnitude of the task militated against the fulfillment of his good intentions but inspired successors in the *Annales* School, such as Emmanuel Le Roy Ladurie, who wrote about peasants and rural civilization. His book *Montaillou: The Promised Land of Error* (1975) employed the records of the Inquisition innovatively and depicted everyday life and culture in a French village inclined toward religious heresy early in the fourteenth century.

In the United States, the impact of the Second World War and its Cold War aftermath shook the foundations of Progressive historiography. Indeed, successive cataclysmic horrors—ferocious fighting, genocide, and atomic blasts—instilled new appreciation for indeterminacy and uncertainty. Simple verities lost persuasiveness. As Reinhold Niebuhr explained in *The Irony of American History* (1952), even the best of intentions can go awry, resulting in errors and excesses. The Progressive school's commitment to plain dualities, the juxtaposition of selfish business interests against the democratic will of the people, appeared less credible, and as a consequence new ornate and more problematic conceptions of historical realities came to the fore.

The publication in 1945 of Arthur M. Schlesinger's *The Age of Jackson* became monument to Progressive historiography. It developed an argument favoring the continuity of reform as the savior of American politics but with an intriguing twist. Instead of finding the impetus among agrarians and Westerners, Schlesinger located it among urban workers and Eastern liberals. Schlesinger's book set off a flurry of research, writing, and reevaluation. Although some scholars still operated within the context of the Progressive tradition, notably Merrill Jensen in his study of the Articles of Confederation, *The New Nation* (1950), and Eric F. Goldman in his work on reform movements since 1870, *Rendezvous with Destiny* (1952), postwar histories took a different view of the American past.

Richard Hofstadter's *The American Political Tradition and the Men Who Made It* (1948) heralded the shift. Widely read and immensely influential, it lamented the current "lack of confidence in the American future" and "the rudderless state of American liberalism." Fearful that the experiences of history had not prepared the American people to respond creatively in the years to come, Hofstadter faulted a traditionally opportunistic style of political leadership, "a democracy of cupidity," and an absence of truly fundamental differences separating liberals from conservatives. Indeed, they agreed upon essentials, such as the legitimacy of profit incentives and private property. The Progressive historians' emphasis on conflict obscured this reality.

Other scholars elaborated on Hofstadter's theme. Many agreed that homogeneity more than disparity marked the American experience and that consensus had more explanatory power than conflict. But they differed over the reasons. In *The Liberal Tradition in America* (1955), Louis Hartz, a political scientist, explained the uniformities by arguing that Lockean assumptions about political reality bound together the American people. Born directly into the modern world, unlike the Europeans, they had no feudal structures and titled nobility from which true conservatism could emerge. In *The Americans: The Colonial Experience* (1958), Daniel Boorstin attributed the cause to the stark, ineluctable, and practical necessities of surviving in the New World, and David M. Potter, in *People of Plenty: Economic Abundance and the American Character* (1954), found it rooted in material conditions.

Historians in postwar America also reacted against the relativistic implications of Progressive historiography and sought methodologies for producing verifiable results. Such scholars looked to the social sciences and quantification techniques. In *The Concept of Jacksonian Democracy* (1961), Lee Benson employed statistical analysis to show why Arthur Schlesinger's categories in *The Age of Jackson* lacked veracity in New York State Schlesinger's put-down of the numbers crunchers: "As a humanist, I am bound to reply . . . that almost all important questions are important precisely because they are not susceptible to quantitative answers."[3]

Quantification and social scientific models first took hold in the "new" economic history. Called "cliometrics" in the United States, this approach purported to employ sophisticated methods. No longer would economic historians describe and explain specific events. Instead, they would attain greater universality by scrutinizing categories of events, aggregates, and group behavior. Among the foremost practitioners, Robert W. Fogel, in a book entitled *Railroads and American Economic Growth: Essays in Econometric History* (1964), made a controversial claim. Seeking to test the thesis that railroads held central importance in the economic development of the United States, Fogel developed carefully framed models to control variables and explore a counterfactual hypothesis: Would the absence of railroads have made any difference? Remarkably, he concluded, no, it would not, because Americans would have found alternative kinds of transportation. In a second book, *Time on the Cross: The Economics of American Negro Slavery* (1974), Fogel and his colleague Stanley L. Engerman stirred up a dispute by presenting "the peculiar institution" contrary to prevailing views, as efficient, profitable, and conducive to a standard of living as high as Northern workers. Critics denounced this conclusion as false and compared it with anti-abolitionist propaganda before the Civil War.

Numbers also took hold elsewhere. Following the lead of the *Annales* School, historians experimented while pursuing total forms of understanding. Statistical analysis became characteristics of the "new" political and social histories, and the tasks of collecting, storing, and processing the data became ever easier because of computers. Collective biographies and minute examinations of election returns yielded demonstrable conclusions about political behavior. The same held true in investigations of the formation of elites, the distribution of property ownership, the degree of social mobility, and the shape of demographic structure. Through the use of population statistics and parish records, historians could calculate rates of marriage, fertility, and mortality. When critics wondered whether such virtuosity really mean much, William O. Aydelotte responded that quantification merely provided "a means of verifying general statements."[4]

Another approach applied psychoanalytical theory. Though less precise than the mathematical approach, this endeavor also strove for deeper forms of understanding. Focusing on individual behavior, it found the wellspring of action in the human psyche, particularly in the conflict between inner drives and outer constraints. For orthodox Freudians, the experiences of infancy and the relations with parents and siblings held special importance in shaping the future adult. For example, the unfortunate and much-lamented psychoanalytical biography of Woodrow Wilson by William C. Bullitt and Sigmund Freud, *Thomas Woodrow Wilson: A Psychological Study* (1967), attributed Wilson's deficiencies, notably his need to fail, to his inability as a boy to satisfy the demands of an insatiable father.

Psychohistory, the amalgamation of psychoanalytical theory with history, acquired growing influence in the United States after 1945, in part because of diminished faith in reason and progress and also because of an influx of European experts. Their views won over influential American historians, for example, William Langer of Harvard University, and encouraged the utilization of Freud's findings to plumb the depths of the psyche. According to psychohistorians, a greater awareness of the role of unreason in human behavior would result in better history.

The ensuing scholarly efforts have obtained mixed results. Effective psychohistory requires expertise in two demanding disciplines, but not all adherents have formal training in both. As a result, some individual practitioners have inadvertently produced comic consequences, for example, the claim that the Cuban Missile Crisis of 1962 appeared to President John F. Kennedy as a psychosexual drama in which Russian weapons, seen as phallic symbols, threatened the Western Hemisphere with penetration. In capable hands, psychoanalytical techniques employing theories of character formation have achieved notable results. Examples include Erik H. Erikson's *Young Man Luther* (1958), David H. Donald's *Charles Sumner and the Coming of the Civil War* (1960), and Fawn M. Brodie's *Richard Nixon: The Shaping of His Character* (1981). Yet even expert works raised questions, persuading dubious observers to resist the inflated claims of champions such as Lloyd de Mause, who saw in psychohistory an emerging science of human motivation. Critics mounted attacks from two main directions. They assailed the tendency to reduce history to individual biography, thereby endorsing new versions of the old-fashioned and discredited

Great Man theory of history. They also skeptically appraised the possibility of verifying any of the claims set forth. According to this view, psychohistory required blatant, empathetic leaps into the heads of historical actors and allowed for no believable method of proof. Groundless and theoretical, it offered no means of verification. The body of critical works includes Jacques Barzun's *Clio and the Doctors: PsychoHistory, Quanto-History and History* (1974) and David E. Stannard's *Shrinking History: On Freud and the Failure of Psychohistory* (1980). In contrast, Peter Gay's *Freud for Historians* (1985) argues in favor of psychohistory. Gay, who has formal training in each area, employs psychohistorical techniques in his publications and wrote one of the best biographies of Freud.

Although social science inspired some historians, others in the 1960s harkened back to the traditions of Progressive historiography. Seeking to put political commitment back in their works, they preferred contemporary relevance over scientific detachment and sought to elucidate current issues through historical inquiries. Topics such as foreign affairs, race and gender relations, and the use and abuse of political and economic power became subjects of concern. Obviously reflecting disquiet over the Vietnam War, the civil rights movement, the drive for women's liberation, gay and lesbian rights, and the Watergate affair, historians making up the "New Left" rejected bourgeois history by incorporating perspectives from "the underside"—that is, outlooks representative of class, racial, ethnic, and gender groups previously invisible in traditional accounts. Sometimes harshly critical, New Left historiography usually depicted the established system as rapacious, exploitative, and racist in character, and attributed such shortcoming to the imperative of economic capitalism. New Left historians also rejected claims of "American exceptionalism" according to which the United States outranked the nations of Europe in the magnitude of commitment to moral standards.

New Left revisionism challenged orthodox historiography on many points and raised firestorms of dispute. An early statement by William Appleman Williams in *The Tragedy of American Diplomacy* (1959) overturned traditional interpretations by showing how the need for markets and resources undermined commitments to self-determination. Capitalist proclivities function as important determinants. Building on Williams' work, a group of his students and associates at the University of Wisconsin elaborated upon such themes and became known as the "Wisconsin" school. Walter LaFeber's *The New Empire: An Interpretation of American Expansion, 1860–1898* (1963) set forth an economic interpretation of U.S. expansion during the late nineteenth century, and Lloyd C. Gardner's *Architects of Illusion: Men and Ideas in American Foreign Policy, 1941–1949* (1970) performed the same service for the early Cold War era. As a follow-up in 1993, LaFeber published *The American Search for Opportunity, 1865–1913* (Volume 2 in *The Cambridge History of American Foreign Relations*). It covered the same period as his first and retained its commitment to an economic interpretation. LaFeber also underscored the destabilizing effects of U.S. capitalism when projected into other less-developed countries. Indeed, infusions of capitalist enterprise proved to be the most potent revolutionary impetus during the era.

Such New Left renditions and other efforts inspired by social, cultural, and political change led to searching reevaluations of U.S. history that veered off in many directions. Some historians depicted the economic system as a corporate entity, designed, controlled, and maintained by ruling elites with immense exploitative capabilities. Others explored relationships based on class, race, and gender. Such studies illuminated the experiences of laboring people, ethnic and racial groups, women, children, and families. The tide of publications in the area of gender studies also included significant works on lesbians and gays. Such outcomes, surely provocative and challenging, showed the feasibility of doing history while incorporating attitudes and viewpoints other than those associated with white male elites. They also promoted conceptual fragmentation.

Traditional narratives focused on the activities of white male elites had presumed commonalities of experience and supposed that stories about them spoke for everyone. The newer histories, in contrast, raised questions and insisted upon distinctions. When the civil rights movement in the 1950s and 1960s riveted public attention on race relations in the United States, the initial historical works by and large dealt with the issue as they seemed to whites. This approach never satisfied aggrieved minorities. The black perspective later emerged in important studies such as John W. Blassingame's *The Slave Community: Plantation Life in the Antebellum South* (1972) and Eugene D. Genovese's *Roll, Jordan, Roll: The World the Slaves Made* (1974). These books tried to comprehend the institution of slavery from the inside, that is, by showing how it appeared to and affected black people and how they coped with the circumstances.

Similarly, the writing of women's history posed profound conceptual problems. Women who championed equal rights in the liberation movement properly complained that textbook histories had rendered females invisible through exclusion. They just did not show up. Although a few historians had studied women, the writings consisted of a particular sort, focusing either on great women, such as Joan of Arc or Queen Elizabeth I, or on political activists in the reform and suffrage movements, such as Jane Addams or Eleanor Roosevelt. Critics observed correctly that women had to act like men in order to merit attention.

The new scholarship conveyed a feminist insistence on recovering the life stories of ordinary women and putting them into the historical narrative. Neither "great" nor politically active, such subjects included middle-class women, immigrants, ethnics, and all racial groups. Yet the mere organization of such material presented a puzzle. Traditional historians had derived the very categories in which they thought from the world of males. Chronological schemes based on kingly reigns or presidential administrations, economic cycles, or warfare had nothing intrinsically to do with women. The format of the conventional textbook, in short, had scant relevance. How then to incorporate the history of women?

This question pressed heavily upon scholars and allowed for no single solution. In a groundbreaking book entitled *Woman's Proper Place: A History of Changing Ideals and Practices, 1870 to the Present* (1978), Sheila Rothman suggested one response. For her, the study of women in history required an approach consisting of three parts. First, historians must comprehend the roles and responsibilities assigned to women in any given period. Next, scholars must determine the degree to which various women of different classes and races actually adhered to those demarcations. Last, historical studies must carefully observe the process of change, the shifting definitions of women's proper place over time, and the degrees to which the various categories of women actually complied with them. Books such as *Liberty's Daughters: The Revolutionary Experience of American Woman, 1750–1800* (1980) and *Founding Mothers and Fathers: Gendered Power and the Forming of American Society* (1996) by Mary Beth Norton and *The Girl Problem: Female Sexual Delinquency in New York, 1900–1930* (1995) by Ruth M. Alexander have established models for new kinds of historical writing.

Other forms of feminist inquiry take on theoretical implications by exploring cultural constructions of gender in different historical settings and also the nature and impact of patriarchy. The subordination of women to males holds special importance, especially the cultural means for establishing and legitimating such dominance in the ideological and legal realms. Essays collected by Joan Wallach Scott in *Feminism in History* (1996) and *Gender and the Politics of History* (1999) provide insightful commentaries on goals, strategies, and methodologies. Another revealing work, Bonnie G. Smith's *The Gender of History: Men, Women, and Historical Practice* (1998), shows how conventional historiographical studies have downplayed or omitted the contributions of women. Books composed by women typically do not show up prominently in the established canon. Though often excluded from the intellectual mainstream until recently, women writing about history have done so in memoirs, travel accounts, and historical fiction, in which they affirm their own visions of the past and their role in it. Others such as Athénaïs Michelet and Mary Beard, the wives of Jules and Charles, labored inconspicuously but indispensably as assistants and editors alongside their scholar husbands. Smith's book provides some compensation for previous neglect.

A mounting interest in the constitutive role of culture in understanding the history of women and other subjects has produced intriguing results in recent decades. Derived in part from cultural anthropology and the publications of Clifford Geertz, notably *The Interpretation of Cultures: Selected Essays* (1973), this approach—"the cultural turn"—emphasizes cross-disciplinary techniques and depicts cultural constructs as creations of human beings, designed consciously or unconsciously for the purpose of extricating meaning from their experiences in the world and defending the status quo. As a consequence, notions of gender, class, and race within a cultural context appear more as human products than as absolute categories derived from nature, normality, or necessity. In other words, defined differences among people follow from their own cultural assumptions and practices. Another effect has collapsed traditional distinctions between elite culture (symphonic music) and popular culture (the blues). In either case, the importance presumably stems not so much from snobbish notions of intrinsic value or worth as from the meaningful expression of everyday cultural forms.

For historians, cultural approaches have had special utility in the examination of *mentalités,* that is, worldviews associated with particular people or groups in distinctive times and places. Examples include Carlo Ginzburg's *The Cheese and the Worms: The Cosmos of a Sixteenth-Century Miller* (1976), a study of religious heresy among common people in Italy; Natalie Zemon Davis's *The Return of Martin Guerre* (1983), a look into a hidden world of peasant sentiment and aspiration in France during the early modern period; and Robert Darnton's *The Great Cat Massacre and Other Episodes in French Cultural History* (1984), an illuminating probe into the values, attitudes, and perceptions of artisans and rural folk in the eighteenth century. In a virtuoso performance, Drew Gilpin Faust's brilliantly conceived book, *This Republic of Suffering: Death and the American Civil War* (2008), holds immense explanatory power while examining how the experience and expectation of death on massive scales among soldiers and civilians transformed the country into a republic of shared suffering in which traditional views about the meaning of religion and human existence underwent profound change.

Through the application of similar methods, W. H. T. Beezley in *Judas at the Jockey Club and Other Episodes of Porfirian Mexico* (1987) serves up another example while exploring late nineteenth-century folkways. He describes the evolution of a Good Friday religious custom into a kind of political protest. In a show of agency and resistance, dissidents made Judas Iscariot dolls in the likeness of hated local big shots and political bosses and symbolically exterminated them by burning or blowing them up. In recent times, Beezley claims to have seen in Mexican markets Judas dolls adorned with the face of Ronald Reagan. In theoretical terms, Beezley draws on Antonio Gramsci's idea of "cultural hegemony." An Italian Communist party leader and intellectual whom the Fascists executed, Gramsci insisted that constructed definitions of nation, class, gender, and race have sustained the position of ruling elites by legitimating existing power relationships. Such categorizations often present hierarchical rankings while claiming that one group possesses some kind of superiority over others. Though often construed as the consequence of divine will, natural selection, biological imperatives, emotional make-ups, and intellectual capabilities, such statements have origins in culturally determined belief systems. When confronted with claims that people in one category or another have irrevocable rights to status, authority, wealth, and privilege, historians have an obligation to deconstruct bogus arguments and expose them as human inventions.

In recent times, various conceptual and methodological conundrums have confounded practitioners throughout the discipline of history and to an extent have erected barriers against communication. Highly specialized in their expertise, historians sometimes lament that they have difficulty understanding and appreciating the work of colleagues in other fields. In the 1980s, 1990s, and later, critics with traditionalistic inclinations discerned a crisis within the discipline. Warning against the emphasis on diversity and multiculturalism in human studies, Arthur M. Schlesinger Jr. advised against ever allowing history to degenerate into a form of therapy designed to promote personal self-esteem. Similarly, Theodore S. Hamerow feared that history as a discipline has lost its standing as a unifier of knowledge, and Gertrude Himmelfarb has cautioned against misunderstanding, misconception, and other bad effects when historians shift attention to disadvantaged groups and away from the politically powerful who define established systems. In a judicious, thoughtful book, *Telling the Truth about History* (1994), in many ways a defense of new kinds of social and cultural history, Joyce Appleby, Lynn Hunt, and Margaret Jacob warn, nevertheless, about some of the implications of recent developments, especially the skepticism derived from the application of theories of literary criticism to the study of history. Such efforts have raised disturbing questions about fundamentals such as reason, objectivity, and the knowability of the past, suggesting that historical narratives differ hardly at all from fiction and thereby threatening the truth-telling function of history. More on postmodernism will follow in the postscript.

In reaction against an accelerating sense of intellectual fragmentation and isolation, some historians have called for more emphasis on conceptual integration and new approaches to world history. In the vanguard, William H. McNeill published in 1963 his massive, erudite, groundbreaking book, *The Rise of the West: A History of the Human Community*. It presented an account of human experiences beginning in ancient Mesopotamia and ending in the middle of the twentieth century; it also manifested a driving ambition to make the modern world in all its parts historically understandable. Before McNeill, most historians had concentrated their efforts on Europe and Europeanized regions in the Americas and elsewhere while focusing on high culture, politics, and diplomacy. They left prehistory, antiquity, and non-European places to archeologists, anthropologists, classicalists, linguists, Orientalists, and area specialists. McNeill embraced the whole of world history as his bailiwick and followed the lead of Arnold Toynbee, his mentor. McNeill explained the formation and diffusion of religions, cultures, and technologies, especially those associated with food production and land use. These topics in turn contributed to his understanding of civilizations, in his view, the main components of the human community.

Another integrative conceptualization appears in the "capitalist world system" analysis created by Immanuel Wallerstein. His voluminous, jargon-laden publications took inspiration from Fernand Braudel of the *Annales* school and drew upon the methods of economics and sociology. For Wallerstein, new relationships emerged in the West during the years after 1500 and eventually comprised much of the world in a self-contained, self-sufficient, and ever-changing organizational structure. First dominated by the Dutch, then the English, then the Americans, the system operated with predictable and specialized consistency. The Metropole (Amsterdam, London, New York) functioned successively as the financial centers where decision-making authority resided and economic elites made choices about production, distribution, and so forth. The periphery, in contrast, consisted of outlying regions in Latin America, Asia, and Africa where various resources existed in abundance and provided the raw materials necessary for making finished goods. Viewed by Wallerstein as inherently exploitative, the capitalist world system meant privileges for producers and disadvantages for suppliers, resulting in massive inequities on a global scale. For enthusiasts, Wallerstein's books show how the world really works.

What principles of inclusion and exclusion should world historians employ? How should they separate the significant from the ephemeral and meaningful from the trivial? If they follow the leads of McNeill and Wallerstein, they will organize their material around themes signifying the essential aspects and parts of the human community. Other approaches appear in postcolonial and subaltern studies. These new fields invoked non-European perspectives in attempts to make audible the previously unheard voices of the masses of people who as nonwhite nonelites experienced poverty, oppression, and condescension during the age of empires. When European and Japanese imperial structures collapsed in the years after the Second World War, nationalists in the former colonized regions confronted the challenge of constructing functioning political and economic systems. Disorganization, chaos, and violence often followed, yet at the same time the consequences compelled historians to formulate new ideas and techniques while dealing with the former colonial world. They could no longer just tell stories about British activities in India. They had to bring in the Indians.

The term "postcolonial" carries with it two connotations. The first refers to a chronological period, and the second to a means of analysis or critique. In the era after 1945, nationalist movements introduced a time of transition in which Third World people tried to come to terms with colonial legacies. Discussions of identity, race, and place necessarily followed and produced new linkages among history, literature, anthropology, and psychoanalysis as scholars explored the experiences of persons of color who had not been included in the Eurocentric worldview. How they coped and understood their place in the world became issues of vital importance. "Subaltern studies" began among disenchanted Marxists in India who disliked the traditional emphasis on native elite behavior in nationalist movements. They wanted to shift the emphasis to the masses of people whose contributions to Indian nationalist had gone unnoticed. They created their own Indian version of history from the bottom up.

The state of historical studies at present represents a cacophony of voices produced by clashing stratagems and rival interests and allows for no single synthesis standing for all of us. Indeed, it signifies a profound demographic change among scholars in the profession. No longer dominated by the well-to-do scions of aristocratic, East-Coast families, the practitioners of history as a professional discipline include many historians who made their way into the universities after the Second World War because of the G. I. Bill, the National Defense Education Act, and other such public programs. They comprised within their ranks women and men of modest social origin whose objects of study testified to their diversity. Together, employing many different angles of vision, they now participate in the collective enterprise of writing history. Such tendencies show no sign of dissipating.

Although particularities and divergences of many sorts characterize the craft of history, one thing seems clear. History no longer sets forth common stories that presumably speak for the identity and experience of all readers. For many consumers of history, the narratives centering on the activities of white male elites no longer provide satisfaction, stimulation, or a means to truth. We no longer possess a past commonly agreed upon. Indeed, we have a multiplicity of versions competing for attention and emphasizing alternatively elites and nonelites, men and women, whites and persons of color, and no good way of reconciling all the differences. Though the disparities and incoherencies create terrible predicaments for historians who prize orderliness in their stories, such conditions also aptly express the confusions of the world and the experiences of different people in it. If historians can agree on little else, at least they should rejoice in the realization that they have many true stories to tell about the human past.

RECOMMENDED READINGS

The following titles, highly selective, represent a large body of scholarship. *Historians at Work*, Vol. 3: *Niebuhr to Maitland*, and Vol. 4: *Dilthy to Hofstadter* (New York: Harper and Row, 1975), eds. Peter Gay, Victor G. Wexler, and Gerald J. Cavanaugh, show the shift from the nineteenth to the twentieth century. *Historiography: Ancient, Medieval and Modern*, 2nd ed. (Chicago: University of Chicago Press, 1994), by Ernst Breisach, spells out the details and contains a splendid bibliography. Other books delineate trends and current tendencies, among them, *The Past before Us: Contemporary Historical Writing in the United States* (Ithaca, NY: Cornell University Press, 1980), ed. Michael Kammen; *Historical Studies Today* (New York: W. W. Norton, 1972), eds. Felix Gilbert and Stephen R. Graubard; and *History: The Development of Historical Studies in the United States* (Englewood Cliffs, NJ: Prentice-Hall, 1965), by John Higham, Leonard Krieger, and Felix Gilbert. Marc Bloch's classic discussion of methodology is contained in *The Historian's Craft*, trans. Peter Putnam (New York: Vintage Books, 1953).

Works on specific historians include Richard Hofstadter, *The Progressive Historians: Turner, Beard, Parrington* (New York: Alfred A. Knopf, 1969); Lee Benson, *Turner and Beard: American Historical Writing Reconsidered* (New York: Free Press, 1960); Harvey Wish, ed., *American Historians: A Selection* (New York: Oxford University Press, 1962); and Earl E. Thorpe, *Black Historians: A Critique* (New York: William Morrow, 1971). John Barker, *The Super-Historians: Makers of Our Past* (New York: Charles Scribner's Sons, 1982), contains an essay on W. E. B. Du Bois. The views of Charles A. Beard and Carl Becker are set forth in "That Noble Dream," *American Historical Review*, 41 (Oct. 1935), 74–87; and *Everyman His Own Historian: Essays on History and Politics* (New York: F. S. Crofts, 1935). Other works include Ray Allen Billington, *Frederick Jackson Turner: Historian, Scholar, Teacher* (New York: Oxford University Press, 1973); Carole Fink, *Marc Bloch: A Life in History* (Cambridge: Cambridge University Press, 1989); John Kenyon, *The History Men: The Historical Profession in England since the Renaissance* (Pittsburgh, PA: University of Pittsburgh Press, 1984); and Peter Burke, *The French Historical Revolution: The Annales School, 1929–1989* (Palo Alto, CA: Stanford University Press, 1990). The essays in *Histories: French Constructions of the Past* (New York: New Press, 1995), eds. Lynn Hunt and Jacques Revel, show the main trends in French historical thinking since 1945.

Insights into the ongoing debates over research methods are obtained in *Historical Analysis: Contemporary Approaches to Clio's Craft* (New York: John Wiley, 1978), ed. Richard E. Beringer; *Toward the Scientific Study of History: Selected Essays* (New York: J. B. Lippincott Co., 1972), by Lee Benson; *American Historical Explanations: A Strategy for Grounded Inquiry* (Homewood, IL: Dorsey Press, 1973), by Gene Wise; *A Behavioral Approach to Historical Analysis of Historical Data* (Homewood, IL: Dorsey Press, 1969), eds. D. K. Rowney and J. Q. Graham; *Quantification in History* (Reading, MA: Addison-Wesley, 1971), by William O. Aydelotte; and *Which Road to the Past? Two Views of History* (New Haven, CT: Yale University Press, 1983), by G. R. Elton and Robert W. Fogel. Jacques Barzun, *Clio and the Doctors: PsychoHistory, Quanto-History and History* (Chicago: University of Chicago Press, 1974); and David E. Stannard, *Shrinking History: On Freud and the Failure of Psychohistory* (New York: Oxford University Press, 1980), raise probing questions. Peter Gay, *Freud for Historians* (New York: Oxford University Press, 1985), defends the viability of psychohistory. Ronald Takaki, *A Different Mirror: A History of Multicultural America* (Boston: Little, Brown, 1993), tells the story from the viewpoint of diverse persons of color. Ellen Fitzpatrick's *History's Memory: Writing America's Past, 1880–1980* (Cambridge: Harvard University Press, 2002) considers topics such as the "new" history of the Progressive era, Native American history, class and culture between the world wars, and "the myth" of consensus history.

Introductory commentaries on new directions in social and cultural history, especially conceptions of class, gender, race, appear in Roger Chartier, *Cultural History: Between Practices and Representations*, trans. Lydia G. Cochrane (Ithaca, NY: Cornell University Press, 1988); Lynn Hunt, ed., *The New Cultural History* (Berkeley: University of California Press, 1989); Robert F. Berkhofer Jr., *Beyond the Great Story: History as Text and Discourse* (Cambridge, MA: Belknap Press of Harvard University Press, 1995); Peter Burke, *Varieties of Cultural History* (Ithaca, NY: Cornell University Press, 1997); Anthony Molho and Gordon S. Wood, eds., *Imagined Histories: American Historians Interpret the Past* (Princeton, NJ: Princeton University Press,

1998); Eileen Boris and Nupur Chauduri, eds., *Voices of Women Historians: The Personal, the Political, the Professional* (Bloomington: Indiana University Press, 1999); and Peter Burke, ed., *New Perspectives on Historical Writing*, 2nd ed. (University Park: Pennsylvania State University Press, 2001). *History, Theory, Text: Historians and the Linguistic Turn* (Cambridge: Harvard University Press, 2004) by Elizabeth A. Clark examines many of the implications for historical thinking. Finally Julie des Jardins in *Women and the Historical Enterprise in America: Gender, Race, and the Politics of Memory, 1880–1945* (Chapel Hill: University of North Carolina Press, 2003) provides a discerning assessment of how women have contributed to the writing of history.

On the contemporary "crisis" in history, commentary appears in Theodore S. Hamerow, *Reflections on History and Historians* (Madison: University of Wisconsin Press, 1987); Gertrude Himmelfarb, *The New History and the Old* (Cambridge, MA: Belknap Press of Harvard University Press, 1987); and Thomas Bender, "Wholes and Parts: The Need for Synthesis in American History," *Journal of American History*, 73 (Jun. 1986), 120–36. Arthur M. Schlesinger Jr., *The Disuniting of America* (W. W. Norton, 1992), warns of impending danger when history is looked upon as a kind of therapy to build personal self-esteem. Finally, *Telling the Truth about History* (New York: W. W. Norton, 1994), by Joyce Appleby, Lynn Hunt, and Margaret Jacob, explores the emergence of history as an academic discipline in modern times and addresses many important epistemological issues, including postmodernism. Interested readers also should see Georg G. Iggers, *Historiography in the Twentieth Century: From Scientific Objectivity to the Postmodern Challenge* (Hanover, NH: University Press of New England, 1997); and Richard J. Evans, *In Defense of History* (New York: W. W. Norton, 1997), both of which uphold traditional practices.

Articles on historiography sometimes appear in the *American Historical Review*. Recent issues contain "Annaliste Paradigm? The Geohistorical Structure of Fernand Braudel," 86 (Feb. 1981), by Samuel Kinser; "The Contribution of Women to Modern Historiography in Great Britain, France, and the United States, 1750–1940," 89 (Jun. 1984), by Bonnie Smith; and "Guilt, Redemption, and Writing German History," 88 (Feb. 1983), by Theodore S. Hamerow. The issue entitled *The American Historical Association: The First Hundred Years, 1884–1984*, 89 (October 1984) features these essays: "Historical Consciousness in Nineteenth-Century America," by Dorothy Ross; "Beyond Consensus: Richard Hofstadter and American Historiography," by Daniel Joseph Singal; and "J. Franklin Jameson, Carter G. Woodson, and the Foundations of Black Historiography," by August Meier and Elliott Rudwick. Part IV, "Reflections on the Modern Age," and Part V, "Contexts for the Writing of History," in the *Companion to Historiography* (New York: Routledge, 1997), edited by Michael Bentley, concern significant trends and tendencies in modern times, including questions of class, gender, and race.

7

POSTSCRIPT: CULTURE WARS, POSTMODERNISM, AND OTHER ISSUES

During the 1990s, professional history of the sort favored by most academic historians became embroiled in a series of controversies. Some of them, carried out in the public arena, placed history at the center of rampaging culture wars in the United States. Such encounters usually came about when militant, outspoken, and influential groups that possessed fixed and traditional views about history attacked so-called revisionists for misrepresenting, demeaning, and subverting their preferred and more orthodox accounts of the past. One especially heated altercation developed over a proposed 1995 display at the Smithsonian Institution in Washington, DC, to mark the fiftieth anniversary of the atomic bombing of Hiroshima at the end of the Second World War.

At the same time, a more theoretical conflict caused acrimony among scholars at professional meetings and in learned journals. The source of the conflict emanated from a body of thinking known as postmodernism. This body of opinion unsettled some historians by challenging the precepts upon which they based their work. Indeed, by repudiating Enlightenment conceptions of reason, objectivity, and progress and emphasizing the self-contained nature of all language, postmodern theorists allowed for scant distinction between history and fiction by collapsing the former into the latter. In defense of the truth-telling claims of their discipline, historians as a consequence have felt a need, on the one hand, to instruct historical fundamentalists who insist upon sacred and sacrosanct versions of an unchanging past and, on the other, to persuade unbelieving skeptics who deny its knowability.

Other issues also provoked controversy. History teachers at all levels have a responsibility to determine what they want their students to learn. Is memorizing "the facts" enough? Or is it necessary also to instill a sense for critical and analytical thinking? Such skills do not necessarily lead to sedition. These questions became issues of concern in the United States during the debate over the proposed National History Standards in the early 1990s and also cropped up in other countries such as Great Britain, Japan, Germany, and Russia when professional educators attempted to cope with the effects of unsavory episodes in the past. Among other things, the study of history addresses questions of identity, power, and meaning and unavoidably arouses political differences and partisan debates. Although historians strive for some measure of objectivity, they also show their preferences. Conservatives empathize with ruling elites and the status quo. Radicals favor change and the underclasses. Liberals, in between, like moderate reform as the best way to avoid revolutions.

The Smithsonian Institution moved into the center of the culture wars early in the 1990s when it developed plans for an exhibition featuring the fuselage of the *Enola Gay*, the B-29 airplane that dropped the atomic bomb on Hiroshima on 6 August 1945. The proposed display had obtained the support of Martin Harwit, the museum director, formerly an astrophysicist from Cornell University, and a naturalized U.S. citizen from Czechoslovakia whose family had fled from the Nazis. Harwit had vivid memories of the Second World War and wanted the Smithsonian Institution to take up important questions "that are under public debate."[1] The proposed *Enola Gay* demonstration held promise for this purpose but also entailed certain risks. What kind of an exhibit on atomic warfare could possibly satisfy all viewers?

As historian Peter Novick told an audience on National Public Radio in January 1995, "There are all sorts of different, alternative, and legitimate ways of framing the story of Hiroshima." He explained:

> You can frame it as the veterans appear to want, as the culmination of America's response to unprovoked Japanese aggression. You can frame it as a chapter in the history of white atrocities against nonwhites, as an episode in the escalating barbarization of warfare in the twentieth century. You could talk about it as the opening of the terrifying age of potential nuclear devastation.

In other words, Novick argued, there is no one truth about Hiroshima. Historical accounts are always "radically selective narrativizations of events."[2]

The museum curators wrote a script of more than 300 pages to go along with the display. They sought accuracy, balance, thoroughness, and connectedness with modern scholarship. For example, the opening section criticized the Japanese for pursuing a kind of expansionism "marked by naked aggression and extreme brutality." It also established significant distinctions. For most Americans, according to the proposed narrative, the Pacific war differed from the European conflict in important respects. Because of racism and Pearl Harbor, the fighting against Japan turned into "a war of vengeance." For the Japanese, in contrast, "it was a war to defend their unique culture against Western imperialism." Such claims impressed critics as unacceptable; for them, they were too hard on the United States and too easy on Japan.[3]

The other four parts of the script also caused offense. In the second section entitled "The Decision to Drop the Bomb," the text set forth an accurate but debatable proposition arguing that "alternatives for ending the Pacific war other than an invasion or atomic-bombing were available, but are more obvious in hindsight than they were at the time." Other uncertainties also appeared as unresolved questions. Would the United States have employed the bomb against Germany? Did U.S. leaders unwisely ignore Japanese peace feelers? To what extent, if at all, was the bomb intended to influence Soviet behavior in Europe? Quotations from General Dwight D. Eisenhower and other wartime leaders expressed misgivings about the necessity of using the atomic bomb.

In the third and fourth sections, more fodder for controversy appeared in discussions of the means of "Delivering the Bomb" and the effects at "Ground Zero." The text emphasized the role of Colonel Paul Tibbets, the pilot of the *Enola Gay* who led the mission, as well as the military significance of using the B-29 Superfortress in the air campaigns against Japan and the consequences of the atomic bombing for the people of Hiroshima. The Smithsonian's plans called for the use of various artifacts to illustrate the human effects and the horror. Finally in the last section, "The Legacy of Hiroshima and Nagasaki," the proposed commentary reviewed the events leading to Japan's surrender, the obduracy of Japanese military hardliners who resisted capitulation in spite of Hiroshima and

Nagasaki, and the subsequent collapse of the wartime alliance with the Soviet Union, leading to the onset of the Cold War. The conclusion pointed to ongoing dilemmas and paradoxes during the atomic age, highlighting the obvious: now that the nuclear genie had gotten out of the bottle, no good way existed to put it back in again.

As the narrative took shape early in 1993, leaders at the Smithsonian Institution tried to keep interested observers informed of the contents and to avoid the obvious pitfalls of bias, misrepresentation, and error. A nine-member advisory committee consisting of historians and one combat veteran of the Pacific war provided a critique, cautioning against too celebratory a tone in favor of the United States. Veterans' groups had different reactions. The powerful Air Force Association (AFA), a group of lobbyists, especially reacted with disfavor and became the leader in the ensuing fight. According to John T. Correll, the executive director of the AFA, the Smithsonian Institution had erred egregiously by treating Japan and the United States "as if their participation in the war were morally equivalent." According to Correll, "Japanese aggression and atrocities seem to have no significant place in this account."[4]

As viewed by the AFA and other similar organizations, the proposed exhibition failed to commemorate properly the heroism, suffering, and self-sacrifice of U.S. soldiers and sailors during the Pacific war and by so doing displayed insufficient appreciation. It also showed too much sympathy for the Japanese and defied the conviction of many veterans who believed that President Truman's use of the bomb had saved their lives by making a costly invasion of Japan unnecessary. As a consequence, according to Hubert R. Dagley II, an official of the American Legion, many veterans believed that museum curators and academic historians had defamed them by treating their experiences condescendingly, if indeed not contemptuously. Accordingly, they had scant patience with historical accounts pointing to the vindictiveness of the U.S. war effort or to Truman's alleged efforts to gain leverage over the Soviets through atomic diplomacy. Who, after all, started the war in the first place?

In response, the Smithsonian Institution authorized a variety of changes, modifications, and clarifications in the text but could not satisfy the critics. According to Edward T. Linenthal, one of the historians engaged in the controversy, the museum managers faced attacks on many fronts, "from journalists and media commentators, from Congress, from outraged veterans and citizens angered by news accounts." Indeed, the narrative became "an embattled text, attacked, defended, and endlessly revised in an increasingly embittered atmosphere that revealed more about American cultural politics in the 1990s than about the mission of the *Enola Gay* and the decision to drop the bomb." As Linenthal explained, "What emerged was not only a vitriolic conflict over a museum exhibition but a public relations disaster for the Smithsonian and a real threat to its budget, most of which came from congressionally appropriated funds."

The critics assailed the curators and historians for indulging in "revisionist" and "politically correct" versions of the past and supposedly for rewriting history in ways that altered the true story of the Pacific war. What such criticism tended to miss was the context, that is, an awareness that a debate over the use of the bomb had gone on ever since August 1945, that scholars such as Gar Alperovitz and Barton Bernstein had written extensively about it for twenty-five years, and that the experiences of American servicemen, whatever the magnitude of their heroism, bestowed on them no special insight into the reasons behind the high-level decisions of the Truman administration. In this instance, personal memory and conviction clashed with the standards and techniques of professional historians, and the former won.

In November 1994, forty historians signed a letter of protest against what they characterized as the "historical cleansing" of the Hiroshima script. For them, it was "unconscionable" that "pressures from outside the museum" should prevent the presentation of "a balanced range of the historical scholarship on the issue." But the letter had no effect. On 30 January 1995, the museum canceled the controversial exhibit and replaced it with a smaller display featuring part of the airplane and an abbreviated text. Later in May 1995, Martin Harwit resigned his position as director of the museum, explaining that nothing less would satisfy the critics of the Smithsonian Institution.

In the end, as Linenthal observed, "Everyone believed that memory and history had been abused, and the controversy over the *Enola Gay* became a useful symbol for all sides in the history wars going on in America." For the critics, the outcome represented a victory over subversives and seditionists, that is, politically correct proponents of historical revision who depict the United States as arrogant, oppressive, and racist. For historians and museum curators, in contrast, the episode warned of partisan dangers and possibilities of censorship. They lamented a lost opportunity. Just possibly, visitors at the Smithsonian Institution could have faced up to the complex history embodied by the *Enola Gay*.[5]

Postmodernist theorists also have challenged the way in which historians do their work. If, as the theory holds, Enlightenment ideas about reason, objectivity, and the possibility of progress have no validity and if, in addition, historical accounts differ hardly from fiction, then historians have to face the unwelcome prospect of losing the truth-affirming part of their discipline. Without appropriate techniques of verification and authentication and, indeed, without a knowable past to write about, history could not stand as a legitimate body of knowledge.

Good historians have always known that their narratives employ literary techniques. Telling a coherent story based on evidence requires the exercise of imaginative faculties, which is also demanded of fiction writers. At the same time, historians usually have assumed that their reliance on documents and other artifacts, that is, primary sources, sets them apart by providing a link with an actual, knowable past. To be sure, it no longer exists, but it did once. Primary sources, the surviving records, are not identical with the past but provide some means for obtaining ideas about it. Historians in this respect resemble paleontologists, who try to construct historical images of life forms in the natural world through the use of fossils and imagination.

Postmodernist challenges radiate from highly skeptical forms of philosophical thought, linguistics, and literary criticism. In some measure, "the linguistic turn" represents disenchantment with and mistrust of Western scientific and rationalistic worldviews, typically perceived by postmodernists as justification for the use and abuse of power and authority. For postmodernist dissenters, the very idea of objectivity poses a problem. For them, no observer can ever form statements about anything without the influence of bias, prejudice, self-interest, and personal preference. For them, notions of objectivity in history became doubly objectionable, because there is no object to behold. What we call the past is a construct of pure imagination.

Such contentions have an impressive lineage in European thought. In the nineteenth century, the philosopher Friedrich Nietzsche dismissed history as a form of knowledge on grounds that no objectively verifiable accounts could exist independently of the partialities and inclinations of the historian. In the twentieth century, Claude Lévi Strauss, an anthropologist, called into question claims that Western scientific rationality possessed any intrinsic superiority over mythical forms of thinking. Ferdinand de Saussure, a linguist, developed a complicated analysis holding that language shapes images of reality but does not refer to it. In subsequent elaborations by Michel Foucault, Jacques Derrida, Paul de Man, Roland Barthes, and Hayden White, a conception of language emerged as a self-contained system of signs and symbols, referring to themselves but to nothing outside in physical reality. According to this view, as historiographer Georg G. Iggers explains, "The historian is always the prisoner of the world within which he thinks, and his thoughts and perceptions are conditioned by the categories of the language in which he operates." No escape is possible. The "texts" with which historians work are creations of language, referring to nothing outside. This idea, crucial for postmodernists, applies to both primary and secondary sources. Such texts possess no unambiguous meaning and can be read in many ways. When applied to the study of history, postmodernist claims mean that "in the final analysis every historical work is a literary work which has to be judged by categories of literary criticism."[6]

This line of analysis has assumed prominence in literary theory in France and the United States since the 1960s. By removing the distinction between history and literature and fact and fiction, it eliminates one of the essential parts of Western thought since Aristotle. Hayden White has pointed out and lamented "the reluctance to consider historical narratives as what they most manifestly are: verbal fictions, the contents of which are more *invented* than *found* and the forms of which have more in common with their counterparts in literature than they have with those in the sciences." Similarly, Robert Berkhofer observed, "Because normal historians try to reconcile variant interpretations by *reference* to facts rather than by arguments over the nature of narratives as such, they must presume in practice that factuality possessed some sort of coercive reality." By denying factuality, "contemporary literary theory defies the very intellectual foundations of current historical practice."[7]

This radical critique of traditional historical methodology has taken on high levels of importance in theoretical discussions of history in recent times but has had much less impact on the actual writing of history. Indeed, acceptance of the premises would render the writing of history next to impossible. For most traditional historians, the distinction between truth and falsehood has remained fundamental. They understand that most of their writing takes on narrative form and probably would insist in response to the postmodernist challenge that it possesses a special truth-seeking purpose, intended to recapture parts of a past that really existed. As Roger Chartier established the point, "This reference to a reality pre-existing the historical text and situated outside of it, of which the text has the function of producing an intelligible account . . . is what constitutes history and keeps it different from fable or falsification."[8]

To be sure, conceptions of truth have become complex in recent times. In all likelihood, few historians in the present day would accept notions of absolute scientific objectivity or embrace as a goal the rendering of the past exactly as it was. Moreover, many would concede valid points to the postmodernist position. History devoted exclusively to the activities of white male elites of European extraction established the standard for centuries. Misleading ideological assumptions, often teleological propositions concerned with progress and modernization, have infiltrated the discourses of historical scholarship. Excessive deference to the authority of experts has formed a feature of professional conduct in history and elsewhere. Cultural assumptions and constructs do shape human behavior in countless ways, and the history of the world outside of Europe and the United States should not be told in Western terms. Yet history and fiction are not the same, and historians who abandon the distinction do so at their own risk. Was the Holocaust during the Second World War a real or an imagined event? The claim that it was imagined would probably appeal to Holocaust deniers but would impress most historians as profoundly false and immoral. To them, the Holocaust will appear as the most documented atrocity in world history and therefore requires belief. In the end, the evidence still counts for something.

Such highfalutin theoretical discussions at the ethereal heights of academe have had scant impact on classroom teachers in the public schools who have many fights of their own. Often carrying out their labors in overcrowded and underfunded facilities, they have had to determine what to teach their students and how best to do it. In the United States, local authorities under some kind of state supervision traditionally have made decisions about curricular matters. But then in the 1980s, financially pressed state legislatures became concerned with fiscal accountability and tried to make sure that each dollar invested in education obtained good effects. The preferred methods for achieving such ends depended on the utilization of some kind of testing program and also on the development of formal statements of academic standards.

Initially the ensuing push for academic excellence enjoyed broad bipartisan support. In the 1990 State of the Union address, President George H. W. Bush announced a set of National Education Goals intended to draw out new ideas in education in efforts to produce a more educated citizenry. Among other things, he wanted to insure within a decade that "American students will leave grades four, eight, and twelve having demonstrated competency in challenging subjects including English, mathematics, science, history, and geography." He also hoped that "all students learn to use their minds well, so they may be prepared for responsible citizenship, further learning, and productive employment in our modern economy."[9]

Such goals appeared laudable enough to most observers. During the next two years, leaders in the Bush administration, including Lynn Cheney, the chair of the National Endowment for the Humanities (NEH), effectively moved forward with the program while enjoying the support of "the entire spectrum of the American population" [Nash, 151]. In 1991 a newly created task force chaired by Lynn Cheney endorsed the plan for creating a statement of national history standards. It should include both world and U.S. history and should emphasize interpretation and analysis, not just the facts. The members insisted on an open, consensual process including all constituents. Later in December 1991 the NEH under Lynn Cheney agreed to fund the project with a research grant, thereby officially launching the National History Standards Project [157–58].[10]

In a fascinating and dismaying book entitled *History on Trial: Culture Wars and the Teaching of the Past*, three participants in the project, Gary B. Nash, Charlotte Crabtree, and Ross E. Dunn, reported their version of events during the ensuing debacle. What began as a well-intended effort to provide classroom teachers with a better understanding of developments in professional history during the past half-century in the end turned into a politically charged engagement in the culture wars of the United States. Directed by Charlotte Crabtree and Gary B. Nash, the National Center for History in the Schools at the University of California, Los Angeles, took the lead while assembling a team of professors, teachers, and education specialists to develop the standards. Drawing heavily on recent developments in social and cultural history, they sought to embrace the best and most innovative scholarship of the last generation. They also emphasized inclusiveness. For them, history no longer concerned just dead white guys from Boston. It also incorporated working class people, women, persons of color, gays, and lesbians, in other words all types of humanity who previously had not shown up very conspicuously in textbook narratives. The proposed standards went through several revisions.

Over the course of eight months while operating under the leadership of Crabtree and Nash, participants in the project laid out five fundamental standards for historical thinking:

1. Chronological thinking—understanding the temporal order in which events unfold and knowing how to measure and calculate calendar time.
2. Historical comprehension—understanding the "who, what, when, where, and why" of historical trends and events, and learning how to draw on literature, music, art, maps, primary documents, and mathematical data in the study of history.
3. Historical analysis and interpretation—differentiating between historical facts and interpretation, considering multiple perspectives, evaluating debates among historians, assessing the credibility of historical accounts, and respecting the provisional nature of historical interpretations.
4. Historical research capabilities—developing the skills to gather, organize, analyze, and interpret historical data.
5. Historical issues analysis and decision making—identifying issues that people have confronted in the past and the present, bringing historical perspectives to bear on these issues, considering alternative actions people might have taken, and assessing the consequences of decisions made.[11]

They then divided the course of U.S. history into ten chronological eras and devised thirty-one standards of understanding. For example in Era 1, "Three Worlds Meet (Beginning in 1620)," the standards called for an understanding of "the characteristics of societies in the Americas, western Europe, and West Africa that increasingly interacted after 1450" and of "Early European exploration and colonization; the resulting cultural and ecological interactions." In Era 10, "Contemporary United States (1968 to the present)," the standards required comprehension of "major developments in foreign and domestic policies during the Cold War" and "major social and economic developments in contemporary America." The authors also provided specific questions; for example, in Era 1, "explain the origins and migration from Asia to the Americas" and "compare commonalities and differences between North American and European outlooks." For Era 10, the Standards called upon students to analyze "the Ford and Carter responses to 'the imperial presidency' and to examine "the impact of the 'Reagan Revolution' on federalism and public perceptions of the role of government."[12]

As always, the devil resided in the details, specifically in the choice of examples as illustrations of larger issues. In spite of intense debates among the authors over historiographical issues, including questions of gender, class, race, and multiculturalism, Crabtree and Nash by their own admission had not anticipated the public furor unleashed by the impending publication of the Standards. The uproar began on 20 October 1994 when Lynn Cheney, formerly the chair of NEH, published a scathing editorial in the *Wall Street Journal.* Nash, Crabtree, and Dunn called it "a preemptive strike against the new guidelines." Under a headline proclaiming "The End of History," Cheney denounced the proposed Standards for a variety of reasons. In her words, "Imagine an outline for the teaching of American history in which George Washington makes only a fleeting appearance and is never described as the first president. Or in which the founding of the Sierra Club and the National Organization of Women are considered noteworthy events, but the first gathering of the U.S. Congress is not." She went on to say, "The general drift of the document becomes apparent when one realizes that not a single one of the 31 national standards mentions the Constitution."

Cheney then asserted that the U.S. History Standards embraced a "grim and gloomy" portrayal of topic. She asked, why devote so much attention to the Ku Klux Klan and McCarthyism? According to her, the Standards affirmed "unqualified admiration" for "people, places, and events that are politically correct." Then, in a misrepresentation characteristic of the conservative attack, she cited teaching examples instead of the standards themselves while counting six references to

Harriet Tubman, an escaped slave who rescued other slaves, but found only one mention of Ulysses S. Grant and none of Robert E. Lee. In her view, while downplaying the contributions of white males, the Standards conveyed no grasp of "the spell-binding oratory of such congressional giants as Henry Clay and Daniel Webster, and leave out altogether Alexander Graham Bell, Thomas Edison, Albert Einstein, Jonas Salk, and the Wright brothers."

Cheney asked, "What went wrong?" In response she claimed that Bill Clinton's election to the presidency in 1992 "unleashed the forces of political correctness" and removed any need for revisionist historians "to conceal their great hatred for traditional history." What to do? She wanted to repudiate the Standards or else "much that is significant in our past will disappear from our schools." According to her, the Standards represented the perverted views of an "academic establishment that revels in . . . politicized history."

Four days later, Rush Limbaugh, the radio talk-show host, entered the affray. He told his listeners that the Standards conformed to the America-bashing multicultural agenda of which he had previously warned. According to him, revisionist historians had "bullied their way into power positions in academia" for the purpose of indoctrinating students with the view that "our country is inherently evil." For him the work of a secret cabal, the Standards ought to be flushed "down the sewer of multiculturalism." Ranting on, he claimed, "This country does not deserve the reputation it's getting in multicultural classrooms, and the zenith of this bastardization of American history has been reached with new standards that have been written as part of Goals 2000 to standard- ize history." For him, the standards are "a bunch of p.c. crap."

He then characterized the attributes of proper history. "History is real simple. You know what history is? It's what happened." He went on, "The problem you get into is when guys like this try to skew history by saying. 'Well, let's interpret what happened because maybe we can't find the truth in the facts, or at least we don't like the truth as it's presented. So let's change the interpretation a little bit so that it will be the way we wished it were.' Well, that not what history is. History is what happened, and history ought to be nothing more than the quest to find out what happened."

Such expressions of primitive thinking astonished historians. As Nash, Crabtree, and Dunn observed, they were "by turns, amazed, amused, and aghast at the recent blitzkrieg on the profession's research of the past few decades." As they saw it, historians "have been drawn into a series of public disputes, often reluctantly but also because their own scholarship has precipitated shrill, bombastic argument, especially when it challenged cherished historical narratives." As a consequence, they "have become personalities on the public stage, applying makeup for the TV cameras, miking up for radio talk shows, and writing op-ed essays for local newspapers."[13]

In the ensuing battles of the sound bytes, the scholars operated at a disadvantage. Their responses to polemical attacks appealed for open-mindedness and sometimes required a degree of intellectual subtlety and sometimes fell short in the court of public opinion. For example, Senator Robert Dole of Kansas, then running as a Republican candidate for the presidency, proclaimed that "there is a shocking campaign afoot among educators at all levels—most evident in the national history standards . . . to disparage America and disown the ideas and traditions of the West." In his view, "the purpose of the National History Standards seems not to teach our children certain essential facts about our history, but to denigrate America's story while sanitizing and glorifying other cultures."[14] Running for cover, the Clinton administration refrained from endorsing the National History Standards much as the U.S. Senate.

Other commentators with fairer minds arrived at different conclusions. According to an editorial in the *Minneapolis Star Tribune*, "Cheney, Rush Limbaugh and other detractors of the new standards should be embarrassed." It went on to say, "With a nit-picking focus on whiffs of political correctness, critics like Cheney have missed the new standards' huge contribution—a whole new pedagogy, far more rigorous, challenging and involving than the dates and names approach of past classroom practice . . . School districts that choose to adopt these voluntary standards will discover lively history classrooms full of intense debates far more enlightened than the ones already taking place on talk radio." The *Lincoln Star* of Nebraska averred that "the standards are intellectually demanding . . . They do expect senior high students to begin exploring the shades of truth, to learn the difference between facts and interpretations of those facts." The *Star* embraced the guidelines for promoting "a broader, more thoughtful look at America's past." According to an editorial in the *New York Times*, "Reading the stands and support materials is exhilarating. Students will rejoice in learning from them, teachers will cherish using them."[15]

When at last the controversy dissipated, local school districts and individual teachers all across the United States of course retained the prerogative to employ the Standards in their classrooms, and many did so. For history teachers at all levels, a look at these guidelines can provide energy and ideas for making the study of history come alive. At the same time, the account by Nash, Crabtree, and Dunn provides a reminder that the study of history is inherently divisive. Different people in different places and at different times experience and perceive the past differently. Whether historians should commemorate the past or interpret it according to their own lights will always pose a fundamental problem. As with many issues in the study of history, there seems to be no definitive solution.

RECOMMENDED READINGS

History Wars: The Enola Gay *and Other Battles for the American Past* (New York: Henry Holt, 1996), eds. Edward T. Linenthal and Tom Engelhardt, recounts the controversy at the Smithsonian Institution from the viewpoint of professional scholars. A consideration of the political impact of the proposed National History Standards in the mid-1990s appears in Gary B. Nash, Charlotte Crabtree, and Ross E. Dunn, *History on Trial: Culture Wars and the Teaching of the Past* (New York: Alfred A. Knopf, 1999).

A place to get started on postmodernism is Georg G. Iggers's traditionalistic account, *Historiography in the Twentieth Century: From Scientific Objectivity to the Postmodern Challenge* (Hanover, CT: Wesleyan University Press, 1997). Much more enthusiastically in favor, *The Postmodern History Reader* (London: Routledge, 1997), ed. Keith Jenkins, elucidates some of the implications. Other sympathetic works include Alun Munslow, *Deconstructing History* (New York: Routledge, 1997), and Keith Jenkins, *Why History? Ethnics and Postmodernity* (New York: Routledge, 1999), both of which evaluate positively the thoughts of leading postmodernists, such as Michel Foucault, Jacques Derrida, and Hayden White. Willie Thompson, *What Happened to History?* (London: Pluto Press, 2000) is dubiously critical. *The Killing of History: How a Discipline Is Being Murdered by Literary Critics and Social Critics* (Paddington, Australia: Macleay, 1996) by Keith Windschuttle is a full-scale attack. Also Pauline Marie Rosenau, *Post-Modernism and the Social Sciences: Insight, Inroads, and Intrusions* (Princeton, NJ: Princeton University Press, 1992), is skeptical.

Additional commentary presenting diverse views appears in Lynn Hunt, ed., *The New Cultural History* (Berkeley: University of California Press, 1989); Hayden White, *Topics of Discourse: Essays in Cultural Criticism*

(Baltimore: Johns Hopkins University Press, 1978); Jan Goldstein, ed., *Foucault and the Writing of History* (Oxford, England: Blackwell, 1994); Robert F. Berkhofer Jr., *Beyond the Great Story: History as Text and Discourse* (Cambridge, MA: Belknap Press of Harvard University Press, 1995); and Brian Fay, Philip Pomper, and Richard T. Vann, eds., *History and Theory: Contemporary Readings* (Malden, MA: Blackwell Publishers, 1999). *History, Theory, Text: Historians and the Linguistic Turn* (Cambridge: Harvard University Press, 2004, by Elizabeth A. Clark, provides an illuminating discussion of the implications. *History on Trial: Culture Wars and the Teaching of the Past* (New York: Alfred A. Knopf, 1999), by three authors of the National History Standards, Gary B. Nash, Charlotte Crabtree, and Ross E. Dunn, provides a sympathetic view from the standpoint of historians.

ENDNOTES

1. Edward T. Linenthal and Tom Engelhardt, eds., *History Wars: The Enola Gay and Other Battles for the American Past* (New York: Henry Holt, 1996), 15.
2. Linenthal and Engelhardt, eds., *History Wars*, 28.
3. Ibid., 29ff.
4. Ibid., 35.
5. Ibid., 39, 44, 52, 58, 59.
6. Georg G. Iggers, *Historiography in the Twentieth Century: From Scientific Objectivity to the Postmodern Challenges* (Hanover, CT: Wesleyan University Press, 1997), 9–10.
7. Quoted in Iggers, *Historiography in the Twentieth Century*, 10.
8. Ibid., 12.
9. Gary B. Nash, Charlotte Crabtree, and Ross E. Dunn, *History on Trial: Culture Wars and the Teaching of the Past* (New York: Alfred A. Knopf, 1999), 150.
10. Nash *et al.*, *Culture Wars*, 151, 157–58.
11. Ibid., 177.
12. Gary Nash and Charlotte Crabtree, *National Standards for United States History; Exploring the American Experience, Grades 5-12* (Los Angeles: National Center for History in the Schools, University of California, Los Angeles, 1994), 40, 231.
13. Nash *et al.*, *Culture Wars*, 3–7.
14. Ibid.
15. Ibid., 194–96.

INDEX